St. Croix Island Tourism, USVI

Tour Guide and Tips

Author

Williams Barnes

Copyright Notice

First Printing: 2017.

ISBN: 978-1-912483-15-0

Publisher: Global Print Digital.
Arlington Row, Bibury, Cirencester GL7 5ND
Gloucester
United Kingdom.
Website: www.homeworkoffer.com

Table of Content

Introduction

If St. Thomas is the seasoned older sibling and St. John the dewy beauty, St. Croix is the region's cultural heart. It's an old soul with a lilting bohemian spirit. It also has a population so diverse and multicultural it's been called a "cultural callaloo."

At 84 square miles, St. Croix is certainly the largest U.S. Virgin Island, but it has a small-town feel. That may be because the "plantation island" is a place of bucolic delights, with acres of rural farmland and roads draped in a canopy of mahogany trees. The island's agricultural heritage is undergoing a renaissance: Organic farms in the northwest highlands are flourishing, and a celebrated Agricultural Fair draws thousands of visitors annually. Tied in with this trend is the island's growing reputation as a health-and-wellness destination: St. Croix has more vegan cafes, juice bars, and organic farms than all the other Virgins combined.

But perhaps more than anything, St. Croix is a living museum of the region's tangled past. Much of the architecture from the 18th-century Danish occupancy remains enshrined in picturesque Christiansted, on the island's west end. The colorful Victorian buildings facing the scenic waterfront of the island's second-largest town, Frederiksted, have been revitalized—a fetching welcome mat for the cruise-ship crowds that arrive weekly at the Frederiksted dock.

St. Croix is the most remote and least-visited of the Virgin Islands, separated from St. Thomas and St. John by one of the deepest ocean trenches in the Atlantic. But the island itself is protected by a natural necklace of coral reef, encircling gentle bays and powdery white-sand beaches. If R&R is at the top of your vacation criteria, this may be the spot for you; just ask U.S. Vice-President Joe Biden, who often spends his Christmas holidays in restorative serenity on the island of St. Croix.

History

From its original inhabitants dating back to approximately 2500 B.C. to its exploration and colonization by Europeans, St. Croix has a rich and fascinating history. Historically known for its sugar cultivation, many sugar mill and plantation ruins can be found all across St. Croix as well as the cultural and architectural influences of the seven different countries that have occupied St. Croix. Both the towns of Christiansted and Frederiksted are full of historical buildings and walking tours are offered that include 2 forts, many historic churches, Estate Whim Plantation, and so much more. Join us as we explore and blog about St. Croix History.

St. Croix, the largest of the 50 odd islands, islets and cays that comprise the U.S. Virgin Islands, encompasses 84 square miles and has nearly two-thirds of the territory's land area. With a mean annual temperature of 79.3 degrees, the hottest summer afternoons might climb to 90 degrees, with 99 being the hottest recorded high, and occasional winter nights dropping to below 70, the lowest recorded being 62 degrees. The relative humidity hangs at 80% but is not felt because of the constant breezes coming off the waters.

When Christopher Columbus journeyed west on his second voyage, he sighted the island the Tainos Indians called "Ay Ay" (The River) on November 14, 1493. He anchored off the north shore near a large natural bay west of Christiansted known now as Salt River. In need of fresh water, he sent a landing party ashore. The party attacked the Caribs as they came to greet them in their canoes. The Caribs offered the first resistance by Native Americans to the Europeans that resulted in casualties on both sides.

Originally inhabited about 1900 years ago by wanderers of the Ciboney tribe as they worked themselves north out of South America, the Taino tribes called them the Igneri or Ancient People as they inhabited the island of St. Croix from 650 AD to 1450 AD. However, in 1985, an archaeological site was excavated which proved man was present on the island from 3485BC to 2995 BC. After the Igneri came the Tainos or Arawaks, followed by the Caribs, a fierce tribe who took control in 1425.

Nine hundred fifteen acres, of which 600 acres are underwater, have been set aside at Salt River as a National Park honoring Columbus' landing on St. Croix. The site includes the pre-Colombian habitation area and an ecological preserve. Although Spain originally claimed the island of Santa Cruz, now the French St. Croix, she made little attempt to settle the smaller islands. Most historians agree , Santa Cruz was settled by both the Dutch and English at about the same time, around 1625. The Dutch, along with some French Protestant refugees from the Catholic-dominated portion of St. Christopher (St. Kitts) settled in the harbor area of Bassin, now the present day Christiansted, while the English located themselves on the western part of the island in what is now Frederiksted.

Seven flags have flown over St. Croix, the major ones being Spanish, English, Dutch and French. Privateers, admirals and treasure seekers have all been attracted to the shores, first by the lure of treasure but then by the highly profitable production of cotton, sugar cane, rum, indigo and spices.

By the early 1640's, England and Holland were contending for the islands. As both the English and Dutch settlements expanded, quarreling began between them over territory, jurisdiction and authority of the island. The English Governor on Santa Cruz was killed by the Dutch governor in 1645 and the English settlers retaliated in a furious battle in which the Dutch governor was wounded, and later died of his injuries. The Dutch withdrew from the island and went to St. Eustatius and St. Martin. The French settlers remaining on the island soon departed for Guadeloupe.

The English remained the masters of the island. The colony strengthened and the population increased. The Spanish, on nearby Puerto Rico, were concerned about the growth and in a nighttime maritime attack, comprised of 5 boats and 1200 Spanish soldiers, surprised the English, killing 120 of them and forced the remaining settlers to leave the island. When the Dutch learned of the Spanish overthrow of the English, they landed a small force of men onto the island. They, in turn, were overthrown by the remaining garrison of 60 Spaniards.

The French also heard of the overthrow of the English and seized the opportunity to conquer Santa Cruz from the Spanish in 1650. Philippe de Lonvilliers de Poincy, a strongman official of the Knights of Malta, dispatched 160 of his best troops and succeeded in deceiving the Spanish garrison to capitulate and sail for San Juan. He then promptly sent three hundred planters from St. Christopher to establish, the now renamed, St. Croix.

De Poincy spared no expense nor effort to develop the fertile land of St. Croix. However all imports and exports were detoured through St.

Christopher so he could retain his percentage of the profits. Some of the remaining colonists, in despair and revolt, began illegal trading, smuggling and piracy, which contributed to the lack of progress on the island. The French, then, after three years of their resettling on St. Croix, deeded it to the Knights of Malta, a rich and powerful order of the Roman Catholic Church, in 1653 .

Eventually de Poincy appointed M. du Bois as the Governor to St. Croix, and gave the island tax relief and free trade rights. St. Croix began to prosper under his suggestion that the planters convert their fields from coffee, ginger, indigo and tobacco to the more profitable sugar crops. Bonded labor was first supplied by European men and women who agreed to serve their masters for five to seven years, after which they would be given their liberty. They were carried from island to island and traded amongst the plantation owners.

de Poincy died in 1660 and was succeeded by Chevalier de Sales as Governor of St. Christopher. de Sales made an agreement with the Dominican Order to establish a mission on St. Croix. Seeking to establish even a stronger hold on the island of St. Croix, Louis XIV decided that the Crown should take over the government and commerce through a new commercial company. In 1665 the French West India Company was formed and emissaries we resent from the

King after a contract had been concluded to indemnify the Knights of Malta.

The Company rule did not fare well and lasted only seven years, until 1674,. The King dissolved the Company and replaced it with Crown rule. From 1674, until 1696, illegal trading, wars, privateering, piracy and religious conflicts tore at the Crucian islanders. The Crown then moved 1200 people, including slaves, from St. Croix to St. Dominique (the French part of Hispaniola and later Haiti). Although the French had basically abandoned the island, the island was still claimed by France. King Louis, hearing reports of illegal English settlers on St. Croix, and of pirates using the island as a rendezvous point, considered selling the island to the English for it's half of St. Christopher.

On June 13,1733 the Danish West Indies Company bought the island from France, since most of the French settlers had left the island around 1695, with the stipulation that they would not resell the island without French approval. The Danes discovered an English settlement on St. Croix consisting of 150 Englishmen and 456 workers and resettled the town of Christiansted.. Because of its history and elegant architecture, (most of downtown Christiansted was built with the yellow Dutch bricks that had been used as ballast) the town is a

National Historic Site. Frederiksted was resettled in 1751 and has is own distinctive architectural style.

St. Croix reached a maximum of 264 plantations in 1742 equally divided between cotton and sugar. The 1751 census shows 120 cotton and 122 sugar cane estates. The average size of each plantation was 120 acres, compared to the 60-70 acre plantations of St. Thomas and the 80-90 acres in St. John. The Danes wanted rapid settlement of St. Croix. Surveys done between 1735 and 1753 finally established the boundaries of the plantation estates. The island was divided into 9 quarters and each estate totaled 150 Danish acres. A road through the center of the island, Centerline Road, which still exists and in use today, was used as the base for establishing the pattern of estates. Many of the names of those plantations still are in use today; Judith's Fancy, Prosperity, Solitude, Catherine's Hope, Morningstar, Rust-of-Twist, and Cotton Valley to name but a few.

The planters on St. Croix frequently complained about the methods of the Company, so much so that, St. Croix was given its own government and administration, separate from St. Thomas and St. John, in 1747. In 1753 the planters of the three islands petitioned the King to buy out the Company, which was concluded in 1754. Company rule came to an end and the Danish West Indies became a royal colony under a new form of government. The Crown designated the most lucrative of the islands - St. Croix - as the new capital for all three islands. Thus, the capital of St. Thomas and St. John was moved from Charlotte Amalie on St. Thomas to Christiansted where it remained until 1871 when it returned to Charlotte Amalie.

Today, visiting St. Croix is quite an adventure. In Christiansted, you can shop the day away through quaint pavilions and arcades filled with shops offering French perfumes, china, crystal, batik clothing, local rum and jewelry featuring local designs such as gold locks and sugar mills. You can go sailing for the day and visit Buck Island, one of the world's finest dive spots and an underwater National Monument. If you are interested in scuba diving, several shops located throughout the island, offer trips to Cane Bay, Salt River, Christiansted Harbor and Buck Island providing you with part or all of your equipment needs. Or have your hotel arrange for a sunset sail or Buck Island Barbecue. St. Croix has many fine hotels and guest houses, both large and small, mostly owned and operated by people who now call St. Croix their home.

Throughout the island you will find excellent dining, or try some local fare. There are many other sights to see, and a selection of other things to do. Try your hand at one of the other sports, such as deep sea fishing. St. Croix boasts two 18 hole golf courses and one 9 hole course. When, and if, you tire of this beautiful island you can day trip to St. John or St. Thomas aboard the seaplane.

Historical Events

Historic Artifacts

Historic Artifacts on Company Street

St. Croix is known by many for it's rich history, there is even an archaeological museum here where you can learn about some of the island's earliest inhabitants. The St. Croix Archaeological Society Museum houses a number of interesting pre-Colombian era artifacts that have been excavated here on St. Croix, but new artifacts from multiple eras are still being uncovered today. In fact, while Company Street was being excavated for infrastructure improvements at the end of 2016, many new artifacts dating back to the early days of Christiansted were uncovered by resident archaeologist David Hayes.

Company Street is one of the main roads in Christiansted, and has been since the town was built in the mid-1700s. Stretching from Fort Christiansvaern to the cemetery gate of St. John's Anglican Church, Company Street was historically a two lane dirt road lined with homes and shops built when the Danish owned St. Croix. David Hayes was the archaeologist that performed the Company Street dig, and he kindly presented his artifact findings to the public which included pieces of clay pipes, shards of china and pottery, bottles, glasses, and other relics from everyday life in the mid-18th century.

Interestingly, the areas of Company Street on which certain artifacts were found indicated the socioeconomic status of the people who lived and worked in that area. On the side of Company Street closer to the cemetery and the Free Gut neighborhood, Mr. Hayes found mostly pottery and a few clay pipe stems, indicating residents of the time were of lower class economic status. Outside Apothecary Hall, closer to Fort Christiansvaern, Mr. Hayes found stemmed wine glasses, the bottoms of Dutch gin bottles, and china, indicating residents of a higher economic class lived on this end of of town

Company Street was also the site of Sunday Market Square. At this market, enslaved peoples that worked the sugar plantations would sell their goods and wares on their only day off, Sunday. As you may have read in our our blog Alexander Hamilton's History on St. Croix, Hamilton's mother's store and residence was located on Company Street, just half a block from the Sunday Market. The goings on at Sunday Market, and in the neighboring Free Gut (an area where slaves who had earned their freedom resided), were an integral part of forming Alexander's social and economical ideals. During the Company Street dig, Mr. Hayes found a lot of Moravian pottery in this area as one would expect based the proximity to both Sunday Market Square and Free Gut.

Opposite the location where Bentix Market stands today, Mr. Hayes found a huge cache of artifacts in a pocket of ash and charcoal about 3 feet below the surface of the road. Recovered in this cache were pieces of china, a tea pot lid, pipe stems, and even some pieces of chamber pots. In this case, Mr. Hayes believes the kitchen of an adjacent building caught fire and, once extinguished, the owners likely dug a hole in the dirt road and dumped the burned and broken items into it. Another interesting historical find was a large brick culvert built to direct water from Company Street all the way down to Water Gut. This culvert was 64" tall, and was constructed in the mid to late 18th century

If you would like to learn more about the history of St. Croix, I would recommend starting with a visit to the the St. Croix Archaeological Society Museum. The museum is located in the Apothecary Hall courtyard on Company Street, and is open on Saturdays from 10am-2pm. You can also visit other historic sites across the island including Salt River Bay National Historical Park and Ecological Preserve, Fort Christiansvaern, Fort Frederik, Estate whim, as well local historic churches, cemeteries, and plantation ruins

Alexander Hamilton's History on St. Croix

With the award-winning musical Hamilton selling out on Broadway, there has been a resurgence in interest about the life of Founding Father Alexander Hamilton. It is commonly known that Hamilton was a delegate to the Constitutional Convention, a major author of the Federalist papers, and the United States' first Secretary of the Treasury. What many are surprised to learn is that Hamilton was actually born in the Caribbean, and lived right here in Christiansted, St. Croix for many of his formative years.

Alexander Hamilton was born on Nevis in 1755* to Rachel Faucette Lavien and James A. Hamilton. However, Alexander Hamilton's history on St. Croix really started back in 1745 when his mother first came to the island. Rachel Faucette was the daughter of physician and planter John Faucette, of French Huguenot ancestry, and Mary, and English woman born in Uppington (or Uppingham). In 1745, Rachel came to St. Croix with her mother to visit her sister and brother-in-law, Ann and James Lytton who owned a sugar plantation located about southwest of Christiansted at No. 9 Company's Quarter, known as Estate Grange. Once on St. Croix, Mary Faucette quickly arranged Rachel's unwilling marriage to Johan Michael Lavien, owner of a 75-acre cotton plantation at No. 12B Company's Quarter.

Lavien was much older man than 16-year-old Rachel and was considered a cruel husband, so by early 1750 Rachel had left her husband and son, Peter. Lavien petitioned the Danish authorities to have his errant wife jailed for her flirtatious behavior and unwillingness to live with him as husband and wife. After several months of imprisonment in Fort Christiansvaern, Lavien had Rachel released, assuming she would have learned her lesson and everything would change for the better. Instead, Rachel left St. Croix and moved to St. Kitts. There, she met and fell in love with a 32-year old Scotsman named James Hamilton, who was working for the mercantile firm of Archibald Ingram in Basseterre. Rachel and James eventually moved to Rachel's old home on Nevis, and the couple had two sons, James Jr. and Alexander.

James Hamilton was sent to St. Croix in May of 1765 to collect a debt on behalf of his employer, and Rachel and their two sons accompanied him. This move to St. Croix would mark the beginning of the most influential and formative years of young Alexander Hamilton's life, and would be the site of several tragedies that would befall him. In January of 1766, just months after the family moved to St. Croix, James Hamilton abandoned Rachel and their two sons. While there remains a lot of speculation about the reason James left his family, Alexander Hamilton's explanation many years later to his uncle was: "...my fathers affairs at a very early day went to wreck; so as to have rendered his situation during the greatest part of his life far from eligible. This state of things occasionned a separation between him and me, when I was very young, and threw me upon the bounty of my mothers relations, some of whom were then wealthy."

The next tragedy struck Alexander Hamilton in 1768 when he and his mother contract yellow fever. While Alexander recovered, his mother succumbed to the fever and died on February 19, 1768, leaving the Hamilton brothers orphaned. After Rachel's death, Alexander and his brother were adopted briefly by their cousin, Peter Lytton. Another tragic blow struck the Hamilton brothers just seventeen months later when Lytton committed suicide and the brothers were separated*; James became an apprentice for a local carpenter, while Alexander was adopted by Nevis merchant Thomas StevensWith James gone, Rachel rented a two story house and supported her family by operating a small store on the first floor selling plantation supplies.

The shop and residence were located in Christiansted at No. 34 Company Street (although there was a temporary move to No. 23 Company Street in 1767). Rachel's store sold plantation staples such as meat, salt fish, flour, rice and apples, which she purchased from her landlord, Thomas Dipnall. The location of Rachel's' store and residence was just half a block from the Sunday Market, where the slaves would use their free Sundays to sell and trade their goods and wares. The goings on at Sunday Market, and in the neighboring Free

Gut (an area where slaves who had earned their freedom resided), were an integral part of forming Alexander's social and economical ideals

At the age of eleven, before his mother's death, Alexander Hamilton was hired by Nicholas Cruger as a clerk at the local import-export mercantile firm of Beekman and Cruger. Alexander worked hard and gained invaluable experience working for Nicholas Cruger and his partner. Hamilton would later refer to his time as a clerk on St. Croix as: "the most useful part of his education." An avid reader most of his life, and a self-educated young man, Alexander later developed an interest in writing. He wrote an essay that was published in the Royal Danish-American Gazette, offering a detailed account of a hurricane which had devastated Christiansted on August 30, 1772. Recognizing his diverse talents, Alexander's employers and additional community supporters, provided him with funds to attend college on the North American mainland. Alexander Hamilton left St. Croix in the fall of 1772, eventually settling in New York just before the outbreak of the Revolutionary War. The rest, as they say, is history

For Crucians and true Hamilton historians, it is important for the world to know that his time on St. Croix became eight of the most influential and formative years of Alexander Hamilton's life. Throughout his career, Hamilton certainly remembered and applied the lessons he had learned on St. Croix, most notably his understanding of international trade, the need for a standardized currency and a sound fiscal policy, and his abolitionist views of slavery. Today, you can still walk in the footsteps of young Alexander Hamilton here in Christiansted. If you are interested in learning more, we highly recommend taking a guided Christiansted walking tour that focuses on Alexander Hamilton. If you are feeling a little adventurous, you can also opt to geocache around historic downtown Christiansted and visit landmarks that were a part of the landscape when Alexander Hamilton lived on St. Croix on a multi-cache tour. In either case, enjoy the unique experience of touring the town that shaped the extraordinary life of Alexander Hamilton

A History of Transfer Day

Transfer Day refers to the day that the Danish West Indies were formally transferred to the United States, becoming the U.S. Virgin Islands. At 4:00pm on March 31, 1917, the United States purchased the Danish West Indies from Denmark for twenty-five million dollars. At that time, a formal ceremony was held here in the islands while simultaneously at the State Department in Washington, D.C., a warrant for twenty-five million dollars was given to Danish Minister Brun. While the transfer took place in 1917, the process of the U.S. obtaining the islands from Denmark had actually started over 50 years earlier during the American Civil War.

During the American Civil War, some of the European maritime powers, including Great Britain and France, supported the Confederacy by closing their ports in the Caribbean to Union shipping. Luckily for the Union, Denmark sympathized with their cause and allowed the Union Navy access to the supply station on St. Thomas in the Danish West Indies. Due to the unfriendly actions of the British Government during this time, Vice Admiral David Porter advised President Abraham Lincoln and Secretary of State William Seward of the strategic value of the Danish West Indies (D.W.I.) as a port for naval repairs and shipping. The first negotiations between the U.S. and Denmark for the purchase of the D.W.I. began on January 7, 1865, and were conducted by Secretary Seward with the full support of President Lincoln. Negotiations stalled when President Lincoln was assassinated, but Secretary Seward was able to restart the negations with Denmark in 1866 after Andrew Johnson became presiden

Over the following year, negotiations went back and forth between the two countries. During these discussions, Denmark disclosed that if they were to sell St. Croix then the sale would have to be approved by the French Government due to a stipulation of the 1733 sales agreement in which Denmark purchased St. Croix from France. The agreement stated that should Denmark choose to sell St. Croix, they must give France the first right of refusal to purchase back the island.

Based on this information, the U.S. elected to purchase only St. Thomas and St. John for seven million five hundred thousand dollars.

A treaty for the sale of St. Thomas and St. John was finally signed by both nations on October 24, 1867; however, the treaty still had to be ratified by the U.S. Congress, the people of St. Thomas and St. John, and both houses of the Danish Parliament. The treaty was passed by the people of St. Thomas and St. John, and in the Danish Parliament, where it was then signed by King Christian IX of Denmark on January 31, 1868. Unfortunately, it was voted against by the U.S. Congress due to a series of epidemics and natural disasters that had struck the islands between 1866 and 1867, including outbreaks of yellow fever, cholera and smallpox, a Category 3 hurricane, an earthquake and a tsunam

Although several attempts were later made by the U.S. to reopen negotiations with Denmark, it was not until 1900, under President McKinley and Secretary of State John Hay, that serious discussions began anew. A new treaty was signed in Washington, D.C. on January 24, 1902, to purchase all three of the D.W.I. for five million dollars. The Senate ratified this treaty on February 19, 1902, during President Theodore Roosevelt's administration. Unfortunately, the Danish

Parliament voted against ratification on October 22, 1902 due to some lingering resentment in Denmark regarding the failed 1867 treaty.

It was World War I that finally led to the successful transfer of the D.W.I. to the United States because the dire economic conditions of the islands due to the war had become a financial drain on the Danish Government. Furthermore, the submarine campaign being waged by the Germans was causing serious concerns regarding the protection of the Panama Canal, so the U.S. had to prevent the islands from falling into German hands. Secretary of State Robert Lansing met with Danish Minister Constantin Brun and signed a treaty agreeing to the sale of the D.W.I. on March 4, 1916. This time around, the treaty was ratified by both countries governments and they were formally exchanged in Washington, D.C. on January 17, 1917

On March 31, 1917 the transfer was officially made in Washington, D.C. when a U.S. Treasury warrant for twenty-five million dollars was presented to Danish Minister Constantin Brun by U.S. Secretary of State Robert Lansing. According to the St. Croix Landmarks Society: "The Secretary of the Treasury, William McAdoo had brought the warrant to the State Department and smilingly explained to the Danish Minister that he had brought the money in the form of a warrant because the actual gold coin would weigh nearly forty-eight tons."

Once the warrant had been given to the Danish Minister, Commander Edwin T

Pollock of the USS Hancock, awaiting word on St. Thomas, was notified via cable and radio that the monies had been paid and he was instructed to receive the islands in the name of the United States. At the same time, a dispatch was sent to then-Governor Henri Konow, also in St. Thomas, that all conditions for the transfer of the D.W.I. to the U.S. had been fulfilled

As soon as the official transfer in Washington, D.C. had been completed, transfer ceremonies were held on St. Thomas and St. Croix. On St. Thomas, a Danish guard of honor from the Cruiser Valkyrien drew up in front of the barracks of Christiansfort and the American honor guard drew up opposite the Danish guard. When Commander Pollock left the USS Hancock, a fifteen gun salute was fired from the Cruiser Valkyrien, which was flying the US flag from her foremast. The same fifteen gun salute was fired from the fort upon the landing of Commander Pollock.

After Governor Konow and Commander Pollock had signed the transfer documents, each returned to their respective honor guards and Governor Konow proclaimed the islands transferred to the United States. The honor guards then presented arms, and the Danish flag (known as the Dannebrog) was lowered while the Danish Royal Anthem was played. A twenty-one gun salute was fired from the fort and the three warships in the harbor. The honor guards then changed places and Commander Pollock proclaimed the islands taken into possession by the United States, and the honor guards presented arms and raised the American Flag while the band from the USS Olympia played "Hail Columbia" and the twenty-one gun salute was then repeated

On St. Croix, ceremonies were performed in both Christiansted and Frederiksted. In Christiansted, at 3:30pm, half a company of Danish Gendarmes, under the command of Captain F.N.C. Fuglede, marched from their barracks on Hospital Street to the wharf and lined up facing Fort Christiansvaern. The Marines, commanded by First Lieutenant Edward A. Willing, then marched up to face the Gendarmes. Each group saluted the other by presenting arms, as the Danish Captain and the American Lieutenant greeted each other with drawn swords. Just before 4:00pm, Government Secretary Will Jacobsen, Police Master Andresen, and the Colonial Council of St. Croix arrived as a group. At the first of four strokes from the Steeple Building clock, the Governor Secretary read the following Royal Act: "By Order of His Majesty the King of Denmark, Commodore Konow, Governor ad-interim of the Danish West Indies, delivers at this moment these islands to the representatives of the United States of America. In conformity with the act the Danish Flag is now taken down from all public buildings." With this, Captain Fuglede gave the command to present arms and lower the Danish flag. As the Danish flag was slowly lowered, the Christiansted Industrial Band played the Danish Royal Anthem. The Gendarmes and Marines shouldered arms and changed places so the American detachment now faced the fort. Lieutenant Willing then ordered the American flag to be raised. Arms were again presented and the American flag was raised while the band played "Hail Columbia

In Frederiksted, the USS Olympia, under command of Captain Bion B. Bierer, arrived around noon. The vessel could not enter Christiansted harbor due to her large draft, so a detachment of Marines were sent to Christiansted by motor vehicles. As the steeple struck 4:00pm, the Police Master read the Royal Proclamation aloud to the Marine and the Gendarmes present in Frederiksted. The Lutheran Minister John Faber then conducted a prayer for the old flag. He gave thanks to God for what good had been accomplished under the Danish flag during the centuries it had waved over the islands. Minister Faber also prayed that shortcomings and mistakes made under the flag be forgotten, and asked God to bless the Danish King, and the Danish nation under the Danish flag in the coming days. He also prayed that in the future God would bestow his blessings upon the islands and their people under the American flag. A twenty-one gun salute was fired, the Danish flag was lowered, and the American flag was hoisted under another twenty-one gun salute.

Now an official territory holiday, Transfer Day is commemorated annually with a military parade and various ceremonies and cultural events across all of the islands. During the commemoration of Transfer Day, please remember the history that shaped the U.S. Virgin Islands and the unique relationship these islands share with the people of Denmark. Let us all come together as one people, not just on Transfer Day, but everyday, to celebrate the past, present and future of our U.S. Virgin Island

Historic Properties: Estate Mt. Washington

If you have ever dreamed of owning a piece of historic property, St. Croix currently has several amazing options available. When "sugar was king" in the Caribbean, St. Croix was scattered with sprawling sugar plantations. As time marched on, many of these plantations were partially destroyed by hurricanes, or were abandoned when the sugar trade ceased, subsequently falling into ruin. Today, many of these historic plantation properties are still privately owned and have been restored, or have had new homes built amongst the ruins. Arguably the most well known and stunning of these properties is Estate Mt. Washington

Nestled in the sub-tropical rainforest on the West End of St. Croix, Mt. Washington was one of the original Danish estates built on the island in the 1700's. Originally a cotton plantation in the 1750's, the plantation thrived during the early to mid-1800's when it converted to growing sugar as its main crop. In its heyday, "Estate Mount Washington" was a 160 acre plantation consisting of the great house, a guest cottage, a managers house, the Tranberg cottage, stables, an animal mill, a molasses cistern and rum factory, a sugar boiling shed, a barrel storage and aging room, a dungeon, two water cisterns, three wells, a water mill, a bell tower, and a plantation village of 17 cottages where the laborers lived. Over time, the great house was lavishly expanded to double its original size, making it approximately 6,000 square feet

While the plantation village remained occupied until the 1930's, a hurricane destroyed the great house in 1899, and was hit again in 1916. With their home in ruins, the occupants fled the plantation and the great house wasn't occupied again until 1986, when the current owners moved in. When the current owners began work on the estate, the rainforest had reclaimed the ruins of the great house, which were discovered buried on the grounds in June of 1984. Over the next two and a half years the jungle landscape was cleared away from the ruins, an archaeological study was completed, and the great house was restored to its former grandeur. The owner's attention to detail and dedication to the authenticity of this historic home is evident at every turn. The home currently houses a renowned collection of the owners' West Indian antiques, which perfectly complimenting the home and setting, making you feel like you have truly stepped back in time - while still offering all the modern conveniences you could want

Over the years the Estate Mt. Washington great house, grounds and ruins have been the background for countless photoshoots of brides and models, films, and catalogs. Mt. Washington has been featured in magazines such as Colonial Homes/Traditional Homes, Gourmet, Architectural Digest, Coastal Living, and British Vogue. The estate has also been the site for a Danish film, and was featured in an episode of The Bachelor. The great house and furniture collection have been featured on the St. Thomas television show Inside Out, as well as photographed in Caribbean Elegance by Michael Connors. On more than one occasion, Mt. Washington has been the centerpiece house on the St. Croix Landmarks Society's House Tours as well as being featured in a major Copenhagen newspaper, and in island publications and websites such as Island News, St. Croix This Week, and right here on GoToStCroix.com.

The Spirited History of Caribbean Rum

Rum has a very long and spirited history. While there are several precursors to rum that span the globe, it is generally accepted that rum was first distilled in the Caribbean in the early to mid-17th century. After its inception, rum became the drink of choice for a wide array of people from plantation slaves to pirates, colonial Americans to the Royal Navy, and even colonial Australians. Today, rum is enjoyed by the masses, and can be found on bar menus and market shelves worldwide. If you are here on St. Croix, visit our two rum distilleries to learn about the history of rum and sample the delicious spirit for yourself.

In its most basic form, rum is an alcoholic beverage made from molasses (or directly from sugarcane juice) by a process of fermentation and distillation. The British Caribbean island of Barbados and French Caribbean island of Martinique are considered to be the birthplaces of rum making back in the 17th century, but rum was produced on many of the Caribbean islands. Caribbean sugar plantations of the time produced an abundance of molasses, the byproduct of the process of making sugar. Sugar was produced by crushing sugar cane, boiling the sugarcane juice, and then leaving the boiled syrup to cure in clay pots.

Then, the molasses would seep out of the pots leaving the sugar behind. While a popular cooking ingredient now, back then molasses was like industrial waste, and for every two pounds of sugar produced one pound of molasses resulted. Luckily, the resourceful plantation slaves discovered that molasses could be transformed into alcohol by mixing it with the liquid skimmed off of cane juice during its initial boiling, and then fermenting the mixture. This became the starting point for distillation and the resulting liquor became known as rum

Aside from the British and French Caribbean, distillation of rum also spread to Europe and Latin America. The New England colonists also produced their own rum to cope with the many issues they encountered on the colonial frontier, most notably boredom, epidemic diseases, and an imbalanced ratio of men to women. The British Caribbean rum industry weakened drastically in the late 18th and early 19th centuries, however, due to the American Revolution, the abolition of the slave trade, slave emancipation, competition from European beet sugar industries, and the rise of whiskey drinking in the newly formed United States. Then, in the mid to late 19th century, the Spanish Caribbean began making rum, and Cuba emerged as one of the largest rum makers in the Caribbean. However, Cold War policies in the U.S. and the embargo resulting from the Cuban Revolution greatly benefited the rum producers in Puerto Rico and the Virgin Islands

Today, the majority of the world's rum production still occurs in the Caribbean and Latin America, although rum is also produced worldwide in countries including: Austria, Spain, Australia, New Zealand, Fiji, the Philippines, India, South Africa, Taiwan, Thailand, Japan, the U.S., and Canada. The U.S. Virgin Island of St. Croix offers two well known distilleries, Cruzan Rum and Captain Morgan Rum (Diageo). The Cruzan Rum distillery was founded here on St. Croix in 1760 and is located on the grounds of the historic sugar plantation Estate Diamond. Talk about history, the Cruzan Rum distillery has been run by the Nelthropp family through eight generations since the early 1800s. Originally distilled on Jamaica, then moved to Puerto Rico in the 1950s, Captain Morgan was acquired by Diageo in 2001 and a new state-of-the-art distillery was built and operating on St. Croix by 2012. Now visitors lucky enough to come to St. Croix can visit both distilleries!

Wherever it may have been produced, throughout its spirited history rum has been a party to the economy, history, politics, literature and more. Rum served as a popular means of economic trade in order to fund many enterprises (illegal and immoral as they may be) such as Triangle Trade slavery, organized crime, and military insurgencies including the American Revolution and Australia's Rum Rebellion. In fact, the term "rum runners" was coined to describe those that illegally transported or smuggled alcoholic beverages in areas where such transportation was forbidden by law.

This popular libation also has famous associations, such as its use by the Royal Navy in grog. Grog referred to a drink made from water mixed with rum, used to make stagnant water more palatable on long voyages. Invented by British Vice Admiral Edward Vernon when he commanded a naval squadron in the West Indies, Vernon's 1740 order was that the daily issue of a half pint of rum be mixed with one quart of water and issued in two servings, one before noon and one after the end of the working day. This order became part of the official Royal Navy regulations in 1756, and lasted for more than two centuries! Rum is also synonymous with pirates, hence Captain Morgan Rum being named after Sir Henry Morgan. Sir Henry Morgan started his career as an admiral in the Royal Navy, but made a name for himself as one of the most notorious and successful privateers and buccaneers in history, and one of the most ruthless among those active along the Caribbean's Spanish Main

Rum has come a long way since its invention, and is now produced in various grades and often aged in oak barrels prior to bottling to provide the flavor profile unique to each distillery. In addition to the well known light, dark, and flavored rums, aged and premium rums are also being produced by many distilleries for those with a more discerning palate. My personal favorite is the endless variety of flavored rums, which are perfect for making delicious and refreshing cocktails for the warm days on St. Croix. Both Cruzan and Captain Morgan make flavored rums, and their websites offer dozens of unique cocktail recipes to inspire you. However you enjoy your rum, the sweet flavor, and quintessential pairing of rum with tropical "umbrella" drinks makes rum the spirit of the Caribbean islands' endless summers

Culture

Culture abounds on the island of St. Croix due to its rich history and combination of African, European, Caribbean and American cultures and the people of St. Croix (Crucians) are very proud and happy to share with you. While you're on St. Croix, check out the quadrille dancers, listen to some of the local quelbe or steel drum music, hear storytellers recount legendary St. Croix stories. Depending on the time of year, heck out some of the annual cultural events such as Crucian Carnival, the Agricultural Fair or Mango Melee. Cultural events year-round include Caribbean nights featuring dinner with a local flare followed by the dancing mocko jumbies. There are fun experiences for the whole family, so make sure to incorporate some of the wonderful local culture into your time on St. Croix

Enjoy a Free Waterfront Jazz Concert

There is just something smooth and sultry about jazz that makes it the perfect music for setting a romantic mood. While recorded jazz is great, live jazz is even better. Imagine listening to some live jazz with the one you love, at a historical waterfront venue on St. Croix, as the sun sets over the Caribbean...it doesn't get much more romantic than that!

Some people say that jazz is America's only true art form. Jazz music has a long, rich history originating from the African American culture in the late 19th century and rising to popularity in the mid-1900s, when it captured the attention of romantics across the world. The beauty of jazz music is in its diversity; you can opt for the fast-paced beats of scat jazz, or slow things down with the sultry and smooth rhythm of blues and Motown. Jazz has all the elements that other music has, plus a little something extra. Jazz has the melody of the song, which is the part you're most likely to remember. It has harmony, and it definitely has rhythm (which is really the heartbeat of the song). What sets jazz apart is the improvisation, or ability of jazz musicians make up the music on the spot. Improvisation is an amazing skill unique to jazz musicians. Whatever makes jazz so different, it certainly sets a romantic tone

Here on St. Croix, there are two FREE monthly events where you can enjoy live jazz at sunset: 'Sunset Jazz' in Frederiksted, and 'Jazz in the Park' in Christiansted. On the third Friday of each month, 'Sunset Jazz' is held in Frederiksted at the Buddhoe Park pavilion, just north of the Frederiksted Pier, from 6:00pm until 9:00pm. On the last Friday of each month, from 5:30pm until 7:30pm, 'Jazz in the Park' is held at the bandstand on the lawn of Fort Christiansvaern in downtown Christiansted. Both of these events include an impressive roster of local, Caribbean, and international jazz musicians for your listening pleasure

While the act listening to jazz can be romantic all on its own, you can always up the romance factor to make the sunset jazz events even more memorable. Consider bringing a blanket for you and your special someone to sit on so you can cuddle up together as the soulful sounds of jazz wash over you. As the rhythm of the music begins to move you, embrace the one you love and dance as if no one else was there. As the melodic sounds of the music float across the water, hold hands and go for a stroll to watch the sun set and stars come out. You can also bring some bubbly and snacks and set up a romantic picnic for the two of you to enjoy during the show (or you can buy drinks and food at the vendor tables to support local causes)

Whether you are a resident or a visitor to St. Croix, I highly recommend that you take in at least one of these monthly jazz events. It is an evening of great music in an unforgettable setting. For a romantic evening, bring your someone special and make a date night of it. If you, don't worry not! These events are fun whether you go solo, invite your friends, or even bring your family (since these are both family-friendly events). Remember to bring a blanket or lawn/beach chairs if you want to sit down, or feel free to dance the night away. In honor of the birthplace of jazz, New Orleans: 'Laissez les bon temps roulez' (or 'let the good times roll')!

USVI Celebrates Emancipation in July

Each year the United States of America and her territories celebrate Independence Day with fireworks, patriotic displays, barbecues, picnics and parties. Here in the U.S. Virgin Islands, we get to celebrate not one, but two historical acts of freedom back to back: Emancipation Day and Independence Day. Both Emancipation Day and Independence Day are significant for the freedoms they provided, but took place almost three-quarters of a century apart, and provided different kinds of emancipation to people in different circumstances. Here on St. Croix, we like to take these two days to celebrate the cultural heritage of the island, spend time with family and friends, and enjoy some fireworks of our own.

Most of you reading this know that Independence Day is a federal holiday celebrated by citizens of the USA on the fourth of July. Independence Day commemorates the adoption of the Declaration of Independence on July 4, 1776, in which the Second Continental Congress declared that the thirteen American colonies were now a new nation of their own, the United States of America, and no longer part of the British Empire. The Declaration also established the rights of mankind and the grievances the colonists had against British rule. As a result, Independence Day marks not only the formation of the United States of America, but all of the freedoms it has come to represent for its citizen

On the other hand, many of you may not yet be familiar with Emancipation Day. Here in the US Virgin Islands, Emancipation Day is a public holiday celebrated on the third of July to commemorate the abolition of slavery in the Danish West Indies. The Danish West India Company settled on what is now known as the US Virgin Islands in the 17th century, and brought the trans-Atlantic slave trade to these islands in 1673. Slaves, mainly working on the sugarcane plantations, were forced to work in harsh conditions and treated inhumanely, which lead to several large slave revolts.

Peter von Scholten became governor of the islands in 1835 and attempted to ease the burden of the slaves, but when a non-violent slave revolt broke out on the island of Saint Croix in 1848, led by freed slave and skilled craftsman Moses Gottlieb, (known as 'General Buddhoe'), von Scholten decided to emancipate all slaves. Slavery on the Danish West Indian Islands was officially abolished on July 3, 1848, seventeen years before slavery would be abolished in the USA. The anniversary of this event was declared a territorial public holiday in the US Virgin Islands, and is now often celebrated together with Independence Da

These two holidays give us many wonderful freedoms to celebrate here in the USVI. The largest celebration on St. Croix takes place out in Frederiksted, known locally as 'Freedom City', the site of the 1848 slave revolt that finally brought about the end of slavery in the USVI. Typically held on July 4th, the day's activities include old-fashioned games for children, cultural entertainment, orators and historians, musical entertainment, quadrille dancers, and food, drink and craft vendors. Once the sun has set, fireworks light up the night sky from the Frederiksted Pier and can be seen for miles around

Caribbean Nights: Crucian Culture in Resort Comfort

Visitors to St. Croix often want to know what are considered the "must-dos" of experiencing our beautiful island. While everyone who lives here has their own list of what visitors should do, in almost every case it will include going to Caribbean night at one of the local resorts. Caribbean nights offer a taste of Crucian culture, both literally and figuratively! These family-friendly, weekly events provide delicious Crucian and Caribbean cuisine, fun local and cultural entertainment, and the iconic moko jumbies.

What are moko jumbies? Celebrated as a part of the cultural heritage of the Caribbean, these stilt dancers take pride of place here on St. Croix and throughout the Virgin Islands as the guardians that ward away evil spirits. The important thing to know is that they enthrall both children and adults alike, and you don't want to miss a chance to see them. The good news is that there are three resorts on different parts of St. Croix that offer Caribbean night on different weekdays, so you can choose the one that works best for you and your family

Every Monday night, The Palms at Pelican Cove hosts their Caribbean Night Dinner Show starting at 6pm. Located mid-island on the North Shore, The Palms includes an all-you-can-eat West Indian BBQ buffet featuring BBQ chicken and ribs, as well as local favorites like creole mahi, seasoned rice, and johnny cakes. Watch the waves crash on their award-winning beach and enjoy the sunset from the open air dining area while a local singer and/or band sets the mood with Caribbean-style music.

The real show begins when the moko jumbies enter the dining area on their giant stilts, towering over the guests, and begin to dance. You can sit back and enjoy the show, or get up and dance with one of them, either way you will be amazed at their agility and skill. After the moko jumbies perform, guests are invited to the dance floor to join in some line dancing, led by the eternally fun and friendly staff of The Palms. The finale of the evening's entertainment is CoralFire Entertainment, St. Croix's local fire dancers. These talented artists light up the night with exciting routines choreographed to popular music

Each Thursday night, Divi Carina Bay All-Inclusive Resort & Casino hosts their Caribbean Beach BBQ starting at 6pm. Located on the East End of the island, Divi's Caribbean Beach BBQ is held at The Dockside Restaurant overlooking the South Shore of St. Croix. Enjoy a delicious beach BBQ buffet featuring Caribbean favorites, and listen to the sounds of Caribbean steel pan music. Then, learn how to dance quadrille, the official dance of the U.S. Virgin Islands, with the delightful "We Deh Yah" Cultural Dancers. Finally, the moko jumbies will dance their way onto the floor and wow the crowds with their skills. Make sure to get your picture with the moko jumbies in their colorful costumes, and take a spin around the floor with them (if you are brave enough)!

On Fridays, head to the Renaissance St. Croix Carambola Beach Resort & Spa for their Pirate Buffet & Moko Jumbie Show starting at 6:30pm. Located on the West End of the island, the Pirate Buffet is held at their signature restaurant, Saman, which features ocean-view terrace dining, as well as an inviting indoor area. The bountiful Pirate Buffet includes a carving station, succulent crab, peel-and-eat shrimp, and a myriad of Crucian entrees, salads, appetizers, and desserts. Music sets the mood during dinner, often performed live by local musicians, but the highlight of the evening is the moko jumbies, of course! After the show, stay and dance awhile under the starry Caribbean sky to popular music.

Whichever venue you choose, please make your reservations in advance. You can click on the links included in the "Do More" section below to get the phone number and contact information for all three resorts. Also, if you enjoy the show (which you undoubtedly will) please make sure to tip the moko jumbies and other performers to show your appreciation. While they make it look easy, they work hard to put on a great show each and every night. Most importantly, have fun and enjoy your taste of Crucian culture!

Dance with a Moko Jumbie!

Moko Jumbies are a cultural icon here on the island of St. Croix, and dancing with one of these talented stilt dancers should be on the top of every visitor's 'must-do' list! Children and adults alike are awed by these unique Caribbean dancers and their amazing displays of agility of skill.

Moko Jumbies have been part of the Virgin Island's cultural heritage for over 200 years, and their origins can be traced to Africa as far back as the 13th and 14th centuries. Moko Jumbies are said to ward away evil spirits (or 'jumbies') from parades, gatherings, and festivals by standing on 10-20 foot high stilts, making them tall enough to reach the evil spirits and drive them away from the crowd. Moko Jumbies are generally covered from head to toe in elaborate costumes, hats, gloves, and masks. The story goes, that the Moko Jumbie must be completely covered (except for their eyes) so that the jumbies don't recognize them.

Today, Moko Jumbies have become an integral part of St. Croix's events and cultural scene. You can find the Moko Jumbies welcoming cruise ship passengers at the Frederiksted Pier, leading parades, dancing at jump ups, and as the premier entertainment at many island celebrations. These towering artists perform amazing dances on their stilts to festive music, combining almost slow-motion movements and acrobatic feats with synchronized choreography. You really have to see the Moko Jumbies dance to truly appreciate them. Not only do they seem to float across the floor like ghosts at times, but they shimmy, run, jump and even hop around on one stilt! The balance of these performers is remarkable, especially when you consider that people are encouraged to dance with the Moko Jumbies. Adults and children alike dance under and around the Moko Jumbies' stilts and take pictures with them, all while the statuesque performers dance and pose to the delight of the audience!

After two years of living on St. Croix, I still don't miss an opportunity to see the Moko Jumbies and I go out and dance with them every chance I get. I also enjoy watching the smiles and pure delight on the faces of the crowd when they see these amazing artists for the first time, especially the kids. Not only is dancing with a Moko Jumbie fun, it is also a one-of-a-kind cultural experience. Plus, it is considered good luck to dance with a Moko Jumbie! Seeing the Moko Jumbies is fun and exciting entertainment for the entire family, and can be experienced at weekly cultural nights offered at several hotels and resorts island wide. Please see our Calendar of Events for the dates and locations of the weekly Caribbean nights, as well as the quarterly Christiansted Jump Ups, where you can get your groove on with one of the Moko Jumbies of St. Croix

Travel and Tourism
Adventure

If you are looking for adventure, St. Croix offers a host of options! Whether by land or by sea, the possibilities are endless for the adventurer in you! Land-lover? Enjoy an ATV tour of the rainforest, take a horse back ride on the beach, or seek one of the many geocaches hidden on the island. Looking for something more to do in the turquoise Caribbean waters? Learn to stand up paddle board, take a kayak tour of Salt River, or take a sail boat trip over Buck Island for a snorkel. Whether you prefer hiking or golfing, sportfishing or kitesurfing, St. Croix is an adventure waiting to happen! So, what will you do first?!

Hike to Jack and Isaac Bays

Jack and Isaac Bays are the living embodiment of what you imagine a quintessential Caribbean beach to be, but there is a bit of hike required to get to them. Once you do get there, you will find picturesque beaches of soft, white sand, surrounded by the turquoise Caribbean Sea and a barrier reef teeming with marine life. Even better, the remote nature of these bays provides seclusion which can make you feel like you have the entire beach to yourself.

Located on the very East End side of St. Croix, near Point Udall, Jack and Isaac Bays are comprised of 301 acres of white sand beaches and upland forests, surrounded by a pristine offshore barrier reef. These bays adjoin with a 300 acre government-owned natural area, the combined effort of which protects the entire eastern tip of St. Croix, including nearly four miles of coastline adjacent to the East End Marine Park, the offshore barrier reef, and other marine systems. Jack Bay and Isaac Bay are accessible only by foot, but the hike is scenic and the beaches are worth the effort

The hike to Jack and Isaac Bays starts at the trailhead near Point Udall, where you will find a small parking lot on your right as you are heading up towards the Millennium Monument. You can park there, but please do not leave valuables in your car. The trailhead starts at the parking lot and leads down towards the water. The first beach you reach along the trail is actually at East End Bay. At that point, turn right and head to the west end of East Bay and take the connecting trail west to the beach at Isaac Bay.

Once you are at Isaac Bay, you can head to the west end of that beach and take the connecting trail heading west again. After a few minutes of heading west on the trail you will turn left on a side trail to the beach at Jack Bay. There will be a few signs along the way to point you in the right direction. The terrain along this hike is considered easy to moderate, and is comprised mostly upland forest, scrub brush, and beaches. The trails are usually clear, and short pants should be okay. Please be aware that there is little to no shade on this hike, so wear sun protection and bring plenty of water

Once you reach Jack and Isaac Bays, I highly recommend doing some snorkeling. The coral reefs in these bays, comprised mainly of elkhorn, staghorn and brain corals, are home to at least 400 species of fish, including parrot fish, blue tangs, four-eyed butterfly fish, trumpetfish, and sergeant majors. Starfish, turtles, nurse sharks, urchins, conch, and a variety of other marine species can be found among the coral and in the surrounding sea grass. While both of these beaches are excellent for swimming and snorkeling, Isaac's Bay Beach has less seaweed and rocks, and deeper water, so it is a more popular snorkeling spot. The water is typically calm, but can be a little choppy sometimes. There can sometimes be some current as well, so be aware of the conditions and your abilities because there are no lifeguards out there

Jack and Isaac Bays beaches are typically a great spot if you're looking to escape and enjoy some privacy. The sand on these beaches is powdery soft, and offers a perfect spot to simply spread out your beach towel and enjoy the Caribbean. These beaches, along with the adjoining East End Bay beach, are also home to the largest nesting populations of green and hawksbill turtles on St. Croix. So, keep an eye out for nesting sea turtles, and the turtle nests themselves, and please be careful not to disturb them

When preparing to hike down to, and spend time at Jack and Isaac Bays please remember to be prepared. There are no amenities on either beach, so bring your own towels, snorkel gear, sun protection. and plenty of water. Just keep in mind that you do have to hike in, so make sure you can comfortably carry whatever you choose to take with you. Take your time and enjoy the hike down to Jack and Isaac Bays, the rolling hills and scenic views are breathtaking. Cool off in the Caribbean Sea when you reach the beaches and take in the natural beauty that St. Croix has to offer

Take a Hike to the Annaly Bay Tide Pools

The Annaly Bay tide pools are a series of large, naturally formed pools found on St. Croix's beautiful North Shore. While accessing these pools is a bit of a challenging hike, it is worth every single step. On your way to the tide pools, you will hike through a portion of the island's rainforest and enjoy breathtaking views of Renaissance St. Croix Carambola Beach Resort, Davis Bay, and the seemingly endless Caribbean Sea. Plan accordingly, and the Annaly Bay tide pools will be a day of scenic hiking, playing in the refreshing Caribbean waters, and soaking up natural beauty that you will never forget.

Before you can enjoy the tide pools themselves, you have to hike down to Annaly Bay. This beautiful hike is approximately 2 miles each way, with the trail beginning at the Renaissance St. Croix Carambola Beach Resort. If you go to the resort, the guard at the entry gate will direct you as to where to park your vehicle, and where the trail begins. There are signs marking the beginning of the hiking trail as you cross a wooden bridge from the paved resort road into the rainforest. The hike is somewhat challenging, but once you get there all that effort will be rewarded. Breathtaking is an understatement. As you hike along the trail, and once you reach the tide pools, you will be fully surrounded by the sights and sounds of nature in all her glory

he hiking trail winds through the lush rainforest where you will likely see millipedes, butterflies, hermit crabs, lizards, huge termite nests, and larger-than-life botanicals. As you hike, make sure to watch where you are stepping because the trail is steep and uneven in areas, and it's often traversed by tree roots. You may also encounter nests of ants, but if you continue to move at a steady pace they shouldn't bother you. As you crest the hill you will have a panoramic view from high above the Renaissance St. Croix Carambola Beach Resort towards the east. Then, the rainforest gives way to open areas of waist-high grass leading down to the rocky beach. The terrain of the trail, especially in the more open areas, can be rough, rocky, or muddy, and the trail can be difficult to find and follow. Make sure to watch your step and stay on the trail by looking for natural trail markings and foot-worn paths

The beach at the end of the trial is comprised of smooth rocks and pebbles instead of sand, and the surf can be quite rough on this beach, so it is not great for swimming. But don't worry, the real draw of taking the time to get to Annaly Bay are the tide pools. At the far west end of the beach you will need to climb over (or 'Spiderman' around) the rocks to get to the tide pools. Luckily, there are many natural hand and foot holds in the rocks for you to use to hold yourself up as you climb around the rock walls of the cliff face to the first tide pool. Please be extremely careful as you traverse the rock walls because the rocks are often sharp, wet and slippery, and the waves break against them where your feet will be resting. Again, just take your time and make sure you are wearing sturdy, non-slip shoes or water socks

Once you make it to the first tide pool, there is a little area of rocky beach where you can leave your backpack and take a dip in the refreshing saltwater. The Annaly Bay tide pools are formed by waves and tide pushing seawater through a small crevice into a basin and trapping it there, thus forming swimming pool-sized tidal pools. Luckily, since the crevice continuously allows water to both enter and exit the basin, the water is prevented from becoming stagnate even though it is seemingly still and calm.

Some of the tide pools reach depths of about 4-5 feet, so you can actually float and swim around inside the pools. The elevated rock walls that form the basin protect the pools from incoming waves by acting a breakwater. As the larger waves break over the rock walls of the basin the water cascades down like a waterfall into the tide pools. Standing underneath the water as it falls over the basin wall is the great way cool off, plus the sound of the waves crashing against the basin is oddly soothing. There are more pools than just the first large one you come to, so you can continue climbing over the rocks to the west to check out the other pools. The pools also make for easy snorkeling if you bring your own gear. You may see colorful tropical fish, crabs, sea urchins, and more

Once you have had your fun and cooled off at the tide pools, you hike back out the same way you came in. I recommend giving yourself plenty of time to make the hike back before it gets dark. There are no lights on the trail, which can make for an unnecessarily dangerous hike back to the resort. While the tide pools are the proverbial pot of gold at the end of the rainbow, the hike itself is beautiful as well. Take some time to explore and enjoy the diverse scenery of the hiking trail as you go

Now, the all-important safety lecture. First, if you have never been to the tide pools I suggest taking a guided tour with a local hiking guide for your first excursion so you know what to expect and how to get there safely. Once you leave the resort area the trail and the tide pools themselves are remote, and there is no cellphone signal. Please take extra care to ensure you are prepared, and take your time as you hike to and from the tide pools in order to prevent injury it's a long way back to civilization. I recommend wearing sturdy shoes and plenty of sunscreen and/or other sun protection, especially since there is very little shade once you reach the tide pools. You will also want to bring lots of drinking water, and maybe a snack or bagged lunch to keep your energy up for the hike back. Do not bring valuables with you just to be safe. If you choose to bring a cellphone or camera to take pictures or video, keep it with you and put it into a bag that will keep it dry if it's not waterproof. Also, please treat the hiking trail and tide pool areas with respect. There are no facilities or trash receptacles, so if you bring it in please take it out with you.

Personally, when I do this hike I wear board shorts and a tank top over a bathing suit, I slather myself in sunscreen, and I wear socks and comfortable tennis shoes for the hike. I also generally wear sunglasses and a hat to keep the sun out of my eyes. I carry a small backpack or dry bag with a pair of water socks (or shoes that I don't mind getting wet when climbing into and around the tide pools), along with extra sunscreen, water, and a few granola bars or bags of trail mix. The tide pool hike is a great morning hike. Not only is it cooler in the morning, but hiking to the tide pools in the morning leaves lots of time to enjoy the pools and hike back out in the afternoon, long before the sun goes down. The Annaly Bay tide pool hike is great for couples, families, even small groups, as long as everyone is prepared and is physically capable of making the hike. The tide pools are one of St. Croix's most popular destinations, and with good reason, so make sure you put them on your to-do list!

Brush Up on Your Bush Skills

Have you ever wondered if you have what it takes to survive in the wild? The idea of learning and practicing survival skills is growing in popularity across the globe, and St. Croix is no exception. Here on the island we refer to the rainforest and uncultivated areas of the island as the 'bush', and many traditional bush skills have been practiced and passed down for generations. So take the opportunity to learn some of these engaging bush skills while you are here.

While most think of St. Croix as white sand beaches and blue Caribbean waters, the island's terrain is actually quite diverse. Ranging from the arid desert-like East End to the rainforest of the West End, St. Croix offers a fair amount of bush in which to learn and practice bush skills. If you are like I was before my first visit to Mount Victory Camp, you may find yourself asking 'what are bush skills'? Think of yourself as being stranded in the rainforest (or anywhere for that matter)...at a bare minimum you would need to be able to find food and water, and build some kind of shelter. Knowing the right bush skills allow you to meet those basic needs, and much more. You can learn to make fire by using friction, or make your own rope or cord using natural fibers from your surroundings. Learn to identify plants that are edible, which plants have medicinal uses, and which have practical uses so they you can gather food from your surroundings. Learn to make basic tools for hunting, fishing, and preparing food so you can feed yourself and your loved ones off the land.

Obviously, you want to learn proper bush skills and techniques from an expert. Luckily, there are several groups of experts here on the island that offer classes, workshops and guided hikes that will teach you some of the most popular and useful bush skills including:

- ✓ Primitive fire making
- ✓ Primitive shelter building
- ✓ Making rope and cord form natural fibers
- ✓ Basket weaving
- ✓ Wild food collection and preparation
- ✓ Wild plant identification and their uses
- ✓ Primitive pottery
- ✓ Stone tool making
- ✓ Bowmaking
- ✓ Tracking and awareness
- ✓ Making spears and nets for fishing

If you truly enjoy camping, and want to make a week of learning bush skills, there are annual week long events such as Bush Skills Caribbean

Rendezvous, Tropical Skills Class, and Calabash Survival Quest. These events offer different levels of primitive bush and survival skills, as well as incorporating some of the ecological, cultural and historical aspects of St. Croix. You and your family can learn bush skills that will help you to survive and thrive from the rainforest, to the farm, to the sea while enjoying the natural beauty of St. Croix.

Aside from the obvious usefulness, learning bush skills builds confidence, teaches self-sufficiency, allows you to reconnect with nature, and it's a great way to meet new people and to spend quality time with friends and family. Tom Brown III, considered to be one of the foremost instructors of primitive technology and primitive wilderness survival, said it best when he said: 'First and foremost, learning primitive living skills helps connect us to the earth. When me make the tools we need from things we gather off the landscape, it affords us an intimate understanding of the beings we share the planet with. We see the many uses of each plant and animal and how they can sustain us. It connects us to the circle of life and death, something we as a species have removed ourselves from.' Don't worry if you are not the 'outdoorsy type', you can take a workshop that is only half a day long and still come out with a new bush skill. However you choose to get started, I highly recommend that you unplug, and get back to basics by learning some bush skills

Take the Helm and Learn to Sail

For many ocean lovers there are few pleasures that rival sailing across the cerulean blue Caribbean Sea. There is just something life affirming about being out on the water with the salt air blowing through your hair, the warm sun on your face, and the marine life swimming alongside you. For me, one thing that makes the whole experience even better is taking the helm yourself and sailing the boat.

Whether you are here on vacation or living on St. Croix, take advantage of the calm, warm waters of the Caribbean Sea and learn to sail. We are very fortunate to have an award-winning sailing operation on the island that offers sailing instruction. You can choose to take three hour lessons that will introduce you to the basics of sailing, or you can go so far as to earn sailing certifications - it all depends on how much you want to learn and how much time you have to spend on your sailing adventure. In either case, Lightheart Sailing & Charters is committed to equipping you with the skills and experience you need to sail safely, joyfully, and confidently. Learn on your own boat (if you are lucky enough to own one), or hop aboard Captain Peter Branning and wife Martha Boston's *Lightheart,* a 2007 Hanse 400e high-aspect ratio sloop equipped with a self-tacking jib, a genoa, and an asymmetrical spinnaker.

For the novice that wants an introduction to sailing, Lightheart Sailing & Charters offers private three hour lessons for 1-2 people. These lessons allow you to move at your own pace, building the skills you need toward confidence, independence and pleasure under sail. Captains Branning and Boston can tailor lessons to match your goals, needs and timing, making them ideal for: new boat owners or soon-to-be owners, new sailors practicing their ASA skills, out-of-practice sailors, experienced sailors wanting to upgrade their skills, or spouses developing skills as a co-captains or mate and captain

If you want to dive into learning to sail and earn an American Sailing Association (ASA) certification, Lightheart Sailing is the best! In fact, the lead instructor is Captain Peter Branning who was named one of the ASA's 'Outstanding Instructors' for 2014, and has over 40 years racing, cruising and coaching sailing teams. You can choose from three different ASA sailing courses including: Basic Keelboat, Coastal Cruising, and Bareboat Charter. Or, if you would like to have a stunning sailing vacation while learning to sail, Lightheart Sailing & Charters offers a combination package in which you sail throughout the northern U.S. and British Virgin Islands, stopping for snorkeling and trips ashore as well as packing in all three ASA courses!

Whichever you choose, you will not regret taking the helm and learning to sail. The experience of learning to sail seems to deepen your connection to the sea, and offers the opportunity for you to harness the power of the wind in your sails to fly across the water. Have fun, learn a new skill, and get a taste of the sailing life. Bo

Snorkel the Buck Island Reef Underwater Trail

Buck Island Reef National Monument offers some of the best snorkeling on St. Croix, as well as a postcard-worthy white sand beach surrounded by magnificently clear blue waters. This natural landscape allows visitors to see unspoiled Caribbean beauty while enjoying some of St. Croix's marine life in its natural habitat. Named #2 on the Coastal Living Magazine 'Top 10 Spots to Snorkel', Buck Island Reef National Monument (or Buck Island as it is known locally) attracts around 50,000 visitors a year many coming to snorkel the picturesque underwater trail.

For those of you who like facts and history, Buck Island Reef National Monument is a 176 acre, uninhabited island about 1.5 miles north of the northeast coast of St. Croix. First established as a protected area by the U.S. Government in 1948, Buck Island was made a U.S. National Monument in 1961 by John F. Kennedy with the intention of preserving what he called: '...one of the finest marine gardens in the

Caribbean Sea.' The Buck Island Reef National Monument was greatly expanded in 2001 by Bill Clinton, but most of the monument area is underwater and includes one of only three underwater trails in the United States.

Now for the fun part...snorkelers can expect a mind-blowing underwater world that is teeming with an abundance of coral, marine fauna fish, and marine life in an array of colors, patterns, shapes and textures. The barrier reef is comprised of giant, branching elkhorn coral that create fortress-like walls that form a lagoon between Buck Island and the surrounding seas. Within the lagoon lies the snorkel trail, where plaques depict and describe the fish and marine flora commonly found in the area. With its 4,554 acre long reef, the Buck Island reef is home to over 250 fish species and a variety of other marine life including green sea turtles, hawksbill sea turtles, spotted eagle rays, lemon sharks, and juvenile reef sharks.

As you meander along the snorkel trail through the large coral formations, you will swim alongside schools of blue tangs, trumpet fish, butterfly fish, parrot fish, and maybe even see some of the larger fish like barracuda or reef sharks. If you have never been snorkeling, or it has been awhile, take one of the many tours and let the guides help you find your way around the trail and get comfortable. Take your time along the trail to appreciate the rainbow of colors and the symphony of sounds the ocean provides in this spot, and try to recognize the magnitude of ecosystem that surrounds you

In addition to the world-class snorkeling, complete your day at Buck Island with a stop on the west end of the island at Turtle Beach, voted one of the world's most beautiful beaches by National Geographic. The soft white sands and aquamarine waters are a relaxing way to round out your trip. While you enjoy the sun and sand, keep an eye out for the endangered brown pelicans and lest terns that call this island home, and watch for turtle nests and hatchlings in nesting season as this is one of many turtle nesting beaches on St. Croix

If you want to head out to Buck Island, I recommend taking one of the guided snorkeling tours. The tour operators are permitted by the National Park Service, and are very knowledgeable and professional. The tour operators will give you snorkel lessons if you need them, and they will provide your gear as part of your trip. Plus, I can say from my personal experience of several of the different tour boats, they will make sure you have a great time! Put on your swimsuit, grab some sun protection, water, and maybe a snack, and hop aboard a Buck Island tour for a fun day of underwater exploratio

Make waves on a Wave Runner

Looking to make some waves here on St. Croix? Then head over to Rainbow Beach and rent a wave runner from West End Water Sports. It's a cool and refreshing way to enjoy the crystal-clear Caribbean waters and to take in the natural beauty the West End of St. Croix offers.

If you are comfortable on a wave runner, you can rent one and take yourself out. West End Water Sports has a huge riding area out in front of Rainbow Beach for you to cruise around at your own speed and check out the scenery. Their riding area offers the beautiful, calm waters the West End is known for, but with no coral reefs or other obstacles to worry about. Let it rip and make some waves, or cruise around at a leisurely pace and look for sea turtles! To make it even more memorable, take a wave runner out late in the day and enjoy the sunset.

West End Water Sports also offers some of the best guided wave runner tours on St. Croix. Even better, they can tailor each tour to fit your group. For the water and speed enthusiasts, they offer a full hour of fast riding and wave jumping! For those who want to cruise around and enjoy the scenery, take a tour of the entire West End of the island including Sandy Point, famous for the filming of the last scene in the movie 'The Shawshank Redemption', and head north around Hamm's Bluff and play in the deep blue waters of the beautiful North Shore.

You can even choose to include a stop at Butler Bay where you can snorkel above a ship wrec

Whether you want to do some extreme wave jumping, calm water cruising, or something in between, West End Water Sports offers a wave runner adventure for everyone! When you are finished with your tour and ready to relax, stop back in to West End Water Sports to rent your beach chairs, umbrellas, snorkel gear, and floats, or enjoy free volleyball, bag toss games, and giant Jenga. Have a wet and wild time on the West End

West End Water Sports offers some of the best jet-ski tours on St. Croix or anywhere for that matter! All tours can be completely tailored to each group. You can do some extreme wave jumping or calm water cruising and everything in between. Covering the entire west end of the island you can cruise around Sandy Point, famous for the filming of the last scene in the movie, "The Shawshank Redemption", and/or cruise around Hamm's Bluff and play in the deep blue water of the beautiful north shore. We can even stop and snorkel above a ship wreck

Location : Frederiksted

Phone : (340) 277-8295

Website : www.wewatersports.com

Jump off the Frederiksted Pier!

A favorite pastime of locals and visitors alike is jumping off the Frederiksted Pier. St. Croix is one of the few places left that allows the public to jump off a working pier, and here on the island it is like a rite of passage. With calm, crystal clear water surrounding it, Frederiksted Pier is a great place to jump in and go for a swim!

As long as there is no cruise ship in port, the public can access the pier which offers a designated area for you to jump from with ladders to make the climb back up to the pier easier. In the designated area you'll be jumping approximately 25 feet down into water that is just as deep. You will love the exhilarating feeling of free falling before splashing into the warm Caribbean Sea. It's liberating, and makes you feel like a kid again. As an added bonus, if you jump wear mask or goggles you will surely see a variety of little tropical fish as you swim back to the ladder to ascend, or you can swim around the pylons and check out the abundance of sponges, coral, and sea life

When you are ready to take the plunge, please be aware that while conditions are usually flat and calm there is no lifeguard or rescue boat, so you are on your own. Please be safe and do not do this in conditions less than perfect. Children will love it with proper adult supervision and discretion. Whether you jump just for the fun it, as the start to a dive around the pier, or to go for a swim or snorkel, enjoy all of the fun and beauty the Frederiksted Pier has to offer!

After you are done jumping off the pier, which will likely happen multiple times, relax on the beach or grab a bite and enjoy the beautiful West End of St. Croix

Bioluminescent Bays of St. Croix

St. Croix is home to not one, but TWO of the Caribbean's rare bioluminescent bays! Both Salt River Bay National Historical Park and Ecological Preserve and Altona Lagoon offer visitors a chance to witness nature's "living lights" at night. For those of you not familiar with this concept, a bioluminescent bay (or bio bay) is a natural occurrence caused by a high concentration of bioluminescent micro-organisms called dinoflagellates.

Depending on the night and location, there are actually three different types of bioluminescent organisms that may be seen: dinoflagellates (the most common), glow worms and/or ctenophora (or comb jelly fish). At night, the dinoflagellates are often seen as tiny sparkles or as individual flashes of light as water is disturbed. In fact, when kayaking through the bio bays, the movement of the kayak through the water makes the dinoflagellates appear like stars flying past you as you move. The comb jelly fish on the other hand light up neon green like a glow stick when they are disturbed with your paddle or touched. And don't worry, comb jellies do not sting so you can touch them, just remember to be gentle because they are VERY fragile creatures!

A combination of factors creates the necessary conditions for bioluminescent bays to form with the most important factor being the presence of red mangrove trees, which surround the Salt River Bay. In fact, research being conducted at the Salt River Bay by the University of South Carolina, the University of North Carolina Wilmington and the University of the Virgin Islands is focused on analyzing the quality and nutrient composition of the bay's water, the distribution of the dinoflagellates, and the abundance of "cysts" (or dormant dinoflagellates) embedded in the sea floor. Bioluminescent bays are extremely rare with "only seven year-round lagoons known to exist in the Caribbean" according to Dr. Michael Latz of the Scripps Institute of Oceanography at the University of California San Diego, an expert on bioluminescent organisms; "Any place that has a bioluminescent bay should cherish it like a natural wonder, like a treasure"

If you have the opportunity, don't miss visiting St. Croix's breathtaking bioluminescent bays. Keep in mind that you can't see bioluminescence every night due to weather conditions and the cycle of the moon, which also determine how vivid the "living lights" will be when they are visible! Whether you are visiting the bio bays by foot or by kayak, check with your local guide or tour company when planning your trip to ensure you find the best time to go. Also, remember to be ecologically responsible when you visit because many of the

Caribbean's bio bays are in danger of having their lights put out permanently! You can do your part when you visit by NOT wearing insect repellent, deodorant, perfumes or sunblock as these can kill the bioluminescence. For additional information, conservation tips and news concerning St. Croix's bio bays, please visit www.savesaltriverbay.com

A Hike through Canaan Gut

The St. Croix Environmental Association (SEA), as part of their mission to provide education and community outreach, offers low or no cost activities that provide opportunities to explore St. Croix and to better get to know our island's environment. We joined them this past weekend on one of their hikes.

We started our trek at Discovery Grove, which is situated at the base of Blue Mountain in Estate Canaan. Our fearless leaders, Ty McRae from BushTribe Eco Adventures and Lynnea Roberts from SEA, led us into the bush. We climbed down into Canaan Gut to begin our hike up the back of Blue Mountain.

A gut is a path where water flows, like a seam or a creak. On St. Croix, rain water flows down the hills during rainy periods and the path s they carve are called guts. When there isn't very much rain, the guts are fairly dry and make ideal hiking trails. These guts harbor an abundance of wildlife. Giant bamboo stands, creeping vines, termite nests, giant kapok trees, orb spiders, locust trees, anoles, sprouting coconuts and many, many, many more

The hike was moderately easy with a gradual slope up the mountain. There were some obstacles to maneuver, large rocks and fallen trees. We were almost completely in the shade for the duration of the hike thanks to the large trees towering overhead which made for a very pleasant temperature. There was plenty to see and explore and Ty took his time explaining what we were seeing and where we were headed. We encountered a couple of old Danish hoes and shards of pottery along our trail, evidence of St. Croix's agricultural past

There is no scenic overlook at the peak of this hike; all of the enjoyment comes from exploring what is seldom seen within the rain forest guts and all they have to offer.

About St. Croix Environmental Association

St. Croix Environmental Association began as a grass roots organization and now has 500+ members. It is a non-profit organization that depends on membership dues, donations and grants to continue their work. SEA is committed to protecting and conserving the beautiful island environment of St. Croix. SEA provides educational programs for kids and adults, sponsors activities to engage both members and non-members and provides leadership for a sustainable environment. In addition to guided hikes, they also offer free snorkeling clinics and photography workshops for school children. To learn more about SEA, their scheduled activities and how you can help preserve St. Croix, please visit their website.

About BushTribe Eco Adventures

BushTribe's focus and passion is taking residents and visitors off the beaten path around St. Croix the path less traveled, if traveled at all. They educate their adventure seekers about local vegetation, wildlife and history along the way. Ty McRae is one of the founders of BushTribe Eco Adventures and his high energy and enthusiasm make him a fun and engaging guide.

Kayak for Kids

An annual event hosted by Lutheran Social Services and benefiting the Queen Louise Home for Children, this fundraiser began in 2000 with a group of friends who kayaked from Cane Bay around Ham's Bluff all the way to Frederiksted beach and raised more than $2,500 that first year. By 2011 the event had grown to raise more than $26,000. Participants can kayak or paddle board one of two courses, the Long Course or the Short Course. The Long Course leaves from Cane Bay

Beach, with a water stop at Ham's Bluff, before heading to Frederiksted Beach. The Short Course departs from Ham's Bay Beach and ends at Frederiksted Beach.

At Frederiksted Beach, the participants are treated to a picnic complete with food, drinks and music all kindly donated by the community. This event is NOT a race, so all experience levels of kayakers and paddler boarders are welcome! However, the participant who collects the highest amount of donations receives a special prize. Other prizes are given away during the raffle, including kayak tours, artwork, jewelry and gift certificates to restaurants, again all kindly donated by the community.

Where:

The Long Course leaves from Cane Bay Beach, with a water stop at Ham's Bluff, before heading to Frederiksted Beach. The Short Course departs from Ham's Bay Beach and ends at Frederiksted Beach.

When:

Generally held on a Sunday in mid-June. For the date and start times for this year's event, please visit our Calendar of Events.

Cost:

Participants pay a fee of $50 per person, and are encouraged to collect donations from the community.

Proceeds Benefit:

The Queen Louise Home for Children, which was founded in 1904 in Frederiksted. It is the only residential foster care home in the United States Virgin Islands. They provide temporary placement to children from birth to twelve years old who have been neglected or abused or have any range of developmental disability. The Home also has an Early Head Start Center which works with at risk infants and pregnant women. Queen Louise Home is staffed by full time childcare workers along with AmeriCorp volunteers. Services include in-house counseling for families and individuals, parenting classes, medical and developmental monitoring, tutoring, infant stimulation, preschool instructions, and follow-up and social services after discharge.

Musical Art

You can enjoy St. Croix's art scene in many different ways such as visiting the galleries and studios of resident artists; taking in one of St. Croix's many annual art exhibits supporting local art groups; or, enjoying one of the many productions the community theatre puts on throughout the year. And, don't miss Art Thursday...a gallery and studio walk through Christiansted that takes place one Thursday night each month with live music and free wine tastings. If you feel like putting your creative side to work, take a scheduled art class or workshop offered at one of several locations throughout the island check our events calendar for details. Come and enjoy the art of St. Croix!

Enjoy a Free Waterfront Jazz Concert

There is just something smooth and sultry about jazz that makes it the perfect music for setting a romantic mood. While recorded jazz is great, live jazz is even better. Imagine listening to some live jazz with the one you love, at a historical waterfront venue on St. Croix, as the sun sets over the Caribbean...it doesn't get much more romantic than that!

Some people say that jazz is America's only true art form. Jazz music has a long, rich history originating from the African American culture in the late 19th century and rising to popularity in the mid-1900s, when it captured the attention of romantics across the world. The beauty of jazz music is in its diversity; you can opt for the fast-paced beats of scat jazz, or slow things down with the sultry and smooth rhythm of blues and Motown. Jazz has all the elements that other music has, plus a little something extra. Jazz has the melody of the song, which is the part you're most likely to remember. It has harmony, and it definitely has rhythm (which is really the heartbeat of the song). What sets jazz apart is the improvisation, or ability of jazz musicians make up the music on the spot. Improvisation is an amazing skill unique to jazz musicians. Whatever makes jazz so different, it certainly sets a romantic tone.

Here on St. Croix, there are two FREE monthly events where you can enjoy live jazz at sunset: 'Sunset Jazz' in Frederiksted, and 'Jazz in the Park' in Christiansted. On the third Friday of each month, 'Sunset Jazz' is held in Frederiksted at the Buddhoe Park pavilion, just north of the Frederiksted Pier, from 6:00pm until 9:00pm. On the last Friday of each month, from 5:30pm until 7:30pm, 'Jazz in the Park' is held at the bandstand on the lawn of Fort Christiansvaern in downtown Christiansted. Both of these events include an impressive roster of local, Caribbean, and international jazz musicians for your listening pleasure.

While the act listening to jazz can be romantic all on its own, you can always up the romance factor to make the sunset jazz events even more memorable. Consider bringing a blanket for you and your special someone to sit on so you can cuddle up together as the soulful sounds of jazz wash over you. As the rhythm of the music begins to move you, embrace the one you love and dance as if no one else was there. As the melodic sounds of the music float across the water, hold hands and go for a stroll to watch the sun set and stars come out. You can also bring some bubbly and snacks and set up a romantic picnic for the two of you to enjoy during the show (or you can buy drinks and food at the vendor tables to support local causes).

Whether you are a resident or a visitor to St. Croix, I highly recommend that you take in at least one of these monthly jazz events. It is an evening of great music in an unforgettable setting. For a romantic evening, bring your someone special and make a date night of it. If you, don't worry not! These events are fun whether you go solo, invite your friends, or even bring your family (since these are both family-friendly events). Remember to bring a blanket or lawn/beach chairs if you want to sit down, or feel free to dance the night away. In honor of the birthplace of jazz, New Orleans: 'Laissez les bon temps roulez' (or 'let the good times roll')!

Take an Art Class and Get Creative

If you are feeling creative, or just looking for something new to try, why not take an art class? The variety of art classes available on St. Croix is constantly expanding and changing, offering endless possibilities of ways to unlock your creativity. Whether you are a novice or you have never taken an art class in your life, there is something for everyone! As an added bonus, taking an art class is a fun way to get out and meet new people in a fun, stress-free environment.

For those of you who have not yet experienced an art class as adult, the thought of trying to create artwork in a room full of people may sound a bit intimidating. Well, fear not! Taking an art class will bring out your inner child and evoke a sense of joy. The classroom environment offers some basic instruction and guidance that can help those of you who think you're not 'creative types' to get those creative juices flowing. Plus, in my personal experiences at The Blue Mutt art classes, everyone in the classroom creates something a little bit different, and everyone is very supportive and encouraging of everyone else

Many people immediately think of painting when they think of art classes. Well, there are, in fact, lots of painting classes available for different skill levels and in different mediums. However, there is an endless amount of creative possibilities, so don't limit yourself to painting. The Blue Mutt, for example, offers classes in making mosaic candle holders, origami, batik fabric, candle making, book/journal making, zentangles, fimo clay, recycled plastic bottle flowers, and mixed media collage. If you need some liquid courage to loosen up and try painting you might enjoy their occasional 'Champain'ting' classes, which include wine or champagne and light hors d'oeuvres as you paint your own masterpiece.

Art classes are available for both adults and children. The cost of the different classes offered at The Blue Mutt vary, but they include the instruction as well as the supplies and materials. The classes change, so check out our Calendar of Events for the current class schedule. You can also have a private 'pARTy' event at The Blue Mutt, which is a fun and unique way to celebrate a birthday or have a girls night out. The very wise Albert Einstein said: 'Creativity is contagious, pass it on.' So, get creative, and pass it on!

Art Thursday: Meet and Mingle with St. Croix Artists

While St. Croix is a small island, it has a large array of artists. From painters and sculptors, to photographers and jewelers, St. Croix is home to many talented artists and designers. Christiansted shines a light on local artists, designers, studios and galleries by hosting Art Thursdays from 5pm to 8pm on the 3rd Thursday of each month from November through May.

On a typical Art Thursday, as you stroll through historic downtown Christiansted you are serenaded by live music while enjoying complimentary wine and refreshments at of many of the local artists' galleries, studios, and shops. This monthly event gives participants a chance to meet the artists, jewelers and designers, while browsing their works. At the same time, Art Thursday affords the galleries and shops a great opportunity to open new exhibits, unveil new design works or feature new artists.

In my opinion, one of the most unique things about St. Croix is getting an opportunity to meet the artist that created the jewelry, photograph or artwork that you are purchasing. It makes the experience of owning an original piece of artwork very personal and memorable. Not to mention that all of the artists have a different inspiration and story behind their creations, and it's fun to get a chance to talk to them about their work and their connection to the island.

Art Thursdays happen monthly from November through May, so head to Christiansted for a fun evening of shopping and socializing that celebrates the wonderful artists that capture the beauty and uniqueness of St. Croix!

Jazz in the Park Christiansted

The last Friday of each month, families of all ages pack a picnic dinner, gather some blankets, lawn chairs and sometimes even the dog and head to lawn at Fort Christianvaern in downtown Christiansted to listen to tantalizing jazz music as the night falls on Christiansted Harbor.

The monthly Jazz in the Park event is hosted by Community Music, Inc., and includes an impressive roster of local and international jazz musicians included the talented Eddie Russell and his jazz band. Located at the bandstand on the lawn at Fort Christianvaern in downtown Christiansted, music lovers spread out on the grass and listen to the musicians play. Admission is free and all families are welcome. The music starts at 5:30 p.m. and continues for two hours. There are public facilities available for use as well. Bring your own food and drinks, or support the local restaurants by dining out before or after the event since the cost for admission is FREE. The relaxing setting is perfect for the whole family: kids can play in grass, parents can kick back on a beach chair or blanket and enjoy the live music in beautiful setting. To confirm that dates,

Supporting Community Theatre

I recently saw my first play at the Caribbean Community Theatre ("CCT")...I was lucky enough to get tickets for the last night of CCT's performance of RENT,which was sold out. While I do love that particular musical, I enjoy all kinds of theatre in general. In my experience it seems that community theatres face a huge challenge in drumming up community support, obtaining sponsors for financial backing and finding talent and volunteers to take part in the productions both on and off stage. As with many community theatres, CCT is a non-profit, volunteer-based organization. Their mission is making theatrical productions available to residents of St. Croix and visitors.

Founded in 1985, CCT produces at least five plays each year in their theater in Orange Grove and past shows have included plays such as: *A Raisin in the Sun, The Odd Couple, Smokey Joe's Cafe, Little Shop of Horrors, South Pacific* and *The Full Monty.*

Tucked up in the Estate Orange Grove neighborhood, cars lined the street on both sides as we found our way to the theatre building. As we approached the doors into the theatre, you could tell just from the crowd gathered outside that the show was very well attended. The staff at the ticket window was friendly and they easily found my tickets that I had ordered online (gotta love technology) and gave them to me along with programs for the show. On the way into the theatre there were raffle tickets for sale, in this particular case they were raffling off a beautiful silver ring with inset stones. Set back in the lounge area down the hall there was also a cash bar where you could purchase red or white wine, some cocktails, water, soda and a few snacks. There were also a few vendor tables selling jewelry, homemade pates, and the like. After indulging in a glass of wine, we headed to our seats to watch the show.

CCT did an amazing job casting and directing the production. The costumes and set were great, and the lights and sound were right on cue. I couldn't believe the talent we have right here on St. Croix! But, what I found to be the most outstanding was the support shown by the community. Everyone was raving about the show, I even talked to one woman who was watching *RENT* for the second time! After the show, the actors and crew came out to the lounge area and mingled with the audience that had stayed after the performance. It was obvious as a newcomer that many of my fellow audience members were regular attendees of CCT, as they hugged the cast and crew members and offered them heartfelt compliments and congratulations on their wonderful performances. You could truly feel the sense of "community" in this community theatre.

Thank you, CCT, for bringing the theatre arts to St. Croix! I look forward to attending many future performances at Caribbean Community Theatre. If you have the opportunity, catch a show or two and show your support for the fine work that CCT is doing! You can also show your support by donating to CCT, or volunteering for future productions. Details are available on their website.

Musicians, Sailors, Hurricane Sandy survivors... perform on St. Croix

A fair amount of musical groups from the mainland tour the Caribbean Islands through the winter. From average to phenomenal, the modes of travel are always the same, though start with flight from said city of origin, make it into Charlotte Amelie' Cyril King airport, and from there it's a mixture of renting vans, hopping puddle jumpers and riding ferries to complete the journey, all the while sleeping in hotel rooms, efficiencies, and crash pads with each new day bringing a different story.

Enter Stell and Snuggs, professional real life musicians, sailors, and troubadours from NYC. Musical partners and lovers, this duo endured losing their home and nearly everything in it through Hurricane Sandy in the fall of 2012 while living in Rockaway Beach, NYC's up and coming hipster con-surf town. After months of organizing food relief for victims with Andrew Wandzilak's (Brooklyn's Two Boots Restaurant owner) brainchild, "Hurricane Sandy Relief Kitchen," which went right along with a lot of couch surfing and sub-leases of their own, this duo decided to take the opportunity of no longer being wed to a home on land to follow a dream that had been brewing for some time to hop aboard a sailing vessel, playing music wherever they go.

Through walls of disbelief and toil, though, they managed to make the 1500 mile sail to the Virgin Islands by way of Bermuda back in November, and have been steadily performing throughout since. Along with them are their two daughters, Arden, 12, and Riley, 3. Along with performing, they homeschool aboard, and hope to provide an enriching experience for their entire family.

Jarad, a brilliant jazz pianist/organist was raised on a healthy dose of bebop, Latin Jazz, and jazz soul from mentors Edward Simon and Trudy Pitts while attending the Philadelphia College of Performing Arts. Rodney Franks of jazz station KUVO 89.3 said, "With his skill and talent on the rise, Jarad Astin continues to grow each and every time he sits at his instrument."

Christel, a classically trained flutist who can switch seamlessly between Bach and traditional Irish music attended the same school where they met in the university choir. "Her runs and articulations are speedy, but nonetheless possessed of a plaintive soulfulness and verve that reminds the listener of an ecstatic nightingale." Rob Wasserman-Colorado Daily

The band is compelling and dynamic, saucy and playful, balancing their performance between instrumental and retro pop songs that they arrange through the sonoric flavorings of the flute, ukelele, piano, and accordion. Stell and Snuggs have drawn from influences further South, such as Brazilian choro and Colombian Cumbia just over the past year. Their music possesses a quality which captures the "all-walks-of-life" listener, as they perform their life experiences through their fingertips.

Sunset Jazz in Frederiksted

On the third Friday of each month, families of all ages pack a picnic dinner, gather some blankets, lawn chairs and sometimes even the dog and head out west to Frederiksted to listen to tantalizing jazz music and watch the setting sun.

Sunset Jazz in Frederiksted has hosted premier Caribbean and International jazz artists from its genesis in 2007. The name has recently been amended to "Sun Set Jazz and More" to the delight of our constant concert goers who, in addition to various forms of Jazz, now enjoy local artists play Quelbe Jazz Fusion, the Sounds of Motown and the Big Band Era. Sunset Jazz is a Frederiksted Economic Development Association (FEDA) event, hosting an impressive roster of local and international jazz musicians on the third Friday of each month. Located at Budhoe Park, just north of the cruise ship pier, music lovers spread out in front of the pavilion where the musicians play. Admission is free and all families, and pets, are welcome. The music starts at 6:00 p.m. and continues until 9:00pm. There are public facilities available for use as well. Just when the sun will slip into the horizon off the waterfront is up to Mother Nature, but it is part and parcel of the evening inspiration.

FEDA operates several cash bars, food vendors provide delectable local snacks and treats. It's easy to support the local vendors when the cost for admission is FREE. The relaxing setting is perfect for the whole family: kids can play, parents can kick back on a beach chair and enjoy the live music in a truly unforgettable setting

Attractions

Historic Attractions, Cultural Attractions, and Natural Attractions. St. Croix has all of them! Make time to visit St. Croix's museums, forts or sugar mill plantation ruins. Sign up for a walking tour through our 2 historic towns of Christiansted and Frederiksted (Twin Cities). Enjoy the natural beauty of St. Croix by checking out the botanical gardens or taking a farm tour in the rainforest. And, no trip to St. Croix would be complete without a rum distillery tour, a day trip to Buck Island, and a visit to Point Udall, the easternmost point of the United States. With all of these attractions, which ones will you choose?!

Benefits of Being a Divi Carina Bay 'Beachcomber'

Divi Carina Bay Beach Resort & Casino is St. Croix's only all-inclusive resort, but you don't have to a visitor on the island to enjoy their facilities. In fact, Divi Carina Bay Casino offers a free players club, the Beachcomber's Gold Club, which not only provides benefits at the casino, but at the resort as well. Both locals and visitors are invite to join the Beachcomber's Gold Club, which offers priority and privileges to its members.

Not a Beachcomber's Gold Club member yet? Good news, it's easy and FREE to join for anyone 21 years or older. Simply present your valid state-issued ID or passport at the Beachcomber's Gold Club at Divi Casino for your personalized account, and you will start earning valuable points immediately. Of course, anyone 21 years or older is invited to enjoy Divi Casino's games and entertainment with no cover charge, but Club members receive added bonuses and benefits for playing such as:

- ✓ Senior members (55+) receive a cash gift every Tuesday and Friday afternoon

- ✓ New members who earn 25 points on their first visit receive a free t-shirt

- ✓ Some months Divi Casino will double or triple your points (more points for free!)

- ✓ Earn a cash gift on your birthday

- ✓ Redeeming points or comps for up to $100 in cash every day

- ✓ Participate in Club promotions like bingo, slot tournaments and cash prize drawings

- ✓ Members who bring in a friend to register for the Club can earn their friend's first-day points

- ✓ A free t-shirt for new members who earn 100 points on their first visit

- ✓ Earn a free meal every Monday and Wednesday

In addition to benefits related to playing at Divi Casino, Club members are also entitled to food, beverage and resort benefits:

- ✓ Enjoy food specials at Carina Café

- ✓ Use your earned points towards the tasty Carina Café, merchandise, specialty drinks, and many things offered at Divi Carina Bay Resort

- ✓ Club members receive a special Divi Carina Bay Resort room rate, including breakfast for two (check with the Club for details)

- ✓ Receive 10% off food or beverages at Divi Carina Bay Resort

- ✓ Receive 10% off activities at Divi Carina Bay Resort, such as mini golf, any non-motorized water sport equipment (paddle boat, peddle board, kayaks), or snorkeling gear rentals

Now that you know the benefits of being a Club member, and how to get signed up, you will want to know how to earn those valuable points. This too is simple, just insert your card into the reader panel on any slot or video poker machine and you will immediately begin earning Club points for your play. Be sure the card reader greets you, if not, re-insert the card or seek assistance from the Beachcomber's Gold Club. You can also earn points while playing table games by simply presenting your Club card prior to each session. Points are earned based upon your average bet and length of play.

On top of all the activities offered at Divi Carina Bay Resort & Casino, Divi Casino also offers great live entertainment every Friday, Saturday, and Sunday night, as well as special events throughout the year. Try your luck, enjoy some live entertainment, and earn some great benefits all at the same time as a Divi Carina Bay Beachcomber!

Location : East End

Phone : (340) 773-PLAY

Website : www.carinabay.com

Self-Guided Tour of Hamilton's Christiansted

For those interested in the life and times of Alexander Hamilton, you should know that the years he spent on St. Croix in the Danish West Indies became eight of the most influential and formative years of his life. Throughout his career, Hamilton applied the knowledge he gained on St. Croix, most notably his understanding of international trade, the need for a standardized currency and a sound fiscal policy, and his abolitionist views of slavery. Today, you can still walk in the footsteps of young Alexander Hamilton here in Christiansted and enjoy the experience of touring the town that shaped his extraordinary life.

The National Park Service (NPS) has researched and prepared a two-page publication/map called *Alexander Hamilton's Christiansted*. This publication offers a self-guided walking tour that will take you around the former capital of the "Danish Islands in America" to some of the sites directly associated with Hamilton's life on St. Croix, when he lived here between the ages of 10 and 18. Here is a list of the sites covered by the NPS self-guided tour:

1. Christiansted Wharf (Christiansted National Historic Site): During the second half of the 1700s, Christiansted was a bustling international port city. Christiansted Wharf was the site of international trade, as well as the wharf at which Hamilton arrived on St. Croix in 1765 as a child and departed from 8 years later to attend school in British North America.

2. Fort Christiansvaern (Christiansted National Historic Site): Hamilton's mother, Rachel Faucette, was imprisoned in the fort for several months in 1750 by her former husband, Johan Michael Lavien.

3. & 4. Numbers 23 and 34 Company Street: Rachel Faucette supported herself and two sons by running a small plantation supply store, which the family resided above. The combination store and residence was located at No. 34 Company Street, but was temporarily moved in 1767 to No. 23 Company Street. Unfortunately, neither structure has survived.

5. St. John's Anglican Church (27 King Street): The Church of England established this parish in 1760 to minister to the growing number of British subjects living on St. Croix. Hamilton's mother, listed as "Rachel Levine", was found in the church's burial records for 1768 after she died from yellow fever. The original wooden church was destroyed in the hurricane of 1772 and was replaced by the existing Gothic revival church in 1780

6. Thomas Stevens' Residence (King Street): After Rachel's death, Hamilton lived with merchant Thomas Stevens and his family on King Street where Hamilton became lifelong friends with Thomas' son, Edward. The exact location of the Stevens' residence is unknown.

7. Former Presbyterian Church (13 Watergut at Prince Street): Reverend Hugh Knox, pastor of the Presbyterian congregation in Christiansted beginning in 1772, befriended Hamilton as a teenager and provided him with religious guidance and helped to further his education. The church property was sold in 1818 and the church building was later demolished.

8. The Firm of Nicholas Cruger (Numbers 7 and 8 King Street): Hamilton went to work as a clerk for the import-export firm of David Beekman and Nicholas Cruger in 1766 at the age of eleven. Hamilton learned the complexities of international trade and foreign exchange while working for Beekman and Cruger and would go on to tell his children that his experiences with Cruger were "the most useful part of his education." Cruger's building was replaced in the late 1700s by the building you see toda

You can pick up a copy of the *Alexander Hamilton's Christiansted* walking tour map and information sheet at the Christiansted National Historic Site's Fort Christiansvaern or the Scale House during their normal business hours. To learn a bit about Hamilton's history in the Caribbean before you set off on a self-guided tour, we recommend reading our blog *Alexander Hamilton's History on St. Croix*. You can also take a guided walking tour of Christiansted that focuses on Alexander Hamilton with CHANT, which is a great way to learn more about how Hamilton's life on St. Croix influenced his education and ideals. Whichever you choose, enjoy strolling some of the streets and sites that Alexander Hamilton walked 250 years ago!

Location : Christiansted

Phone : (340) 277-4834

Website : www.chantvi.org

St. Croix's East End Marine Park

Along with global, local and governmental organizations, the St. Croix community is working to preserve the natural beauty, wildlife, and history of our island. One way St. Croix has worked to achieve this goal is by establishing national parks, protected areas, and wildlife refuges. In addition to being the home of three different national parks managed by the U.S. National Park Service, St. Croix is also home to the first territorial park established in the U.S. Virgin Islands, the St. Croix East End Marine Park (STXEEMP).

Established in 2003 to protect the largest island barrier reef system in the Caribbean, the mission of the STXEEMP is to manage the natural, cultural and environmental resources within the boundaries of the Park. It's a tough job, but someone has to do it in this case it's the VI Department of Planning and Natural Resources (DPNR), Coastal Zone Management. Leading the charge to manage and protect the STXEEMP is the DPNR Marine Park Coordinator, Caroline Pott. When the GOTO Team spoke to Caroline, she explained what is included in the STXEEMP, how DPNR is working to protect the area, and what the biggest challenges have been for the Park. Hilary Lohmann, a NOAA Fellow working alongside Caroline at the Park, also joined us and shared some great information about the park and the supportive non-profit organization, Friends of the East End Marine Park. Based on our discussion, here is what you should know about STXEEMP...

The Park and its Uses:

The waters of STXEEMP envelope the eastern tip of St. Croix and includes 60 square miles of water along 17 miles of shoreline. The boundaries of the Park extend from the high-water mark of the beach to the 3 mile territorial limit, Habitats include seagrass beds, coral reefs, and sandy bottom. The management plan for the park was developed by The Nature Conservancy (as a paid agent of the VI Government) in a collaborative effort with local fishermen and dive operators, professionals at local and national universities, and local and federal agencies. The Park is zoned for multiple uses to accommodate a variety of users while protecting vulnerable and valuable habitats. For those that are not familiar with the different zones and what they mean, here is map and descriptions of the different zones:

- ✓ **Recreation Zone:** Provides areas for snorkeling, diving with a flag, boating, personal watercraft use, and hook-and-line fishing from the shore. Marine Park permits may also be issued for catch-and-release guide fishing and cast-net bait fishing. All other traditional fishing is prohibited.

- ✓ **No Take Zone:** Designed to protect the near-shore environments and encompass large, contiguous, diverse habitats. All fishing, extraction and use of personal watercrafts is prohibited. Diving with a flag, snorkeling, and transit in a boat are all permitted.

- ✓ **Wildlife Preserve:** Intended to protect nesting sea turtles. Activities that may disturb or harm nesting turtles are prohibited in these waters. The Endangered Species Act prohibits harassment, take, or alteration of behavior of sea turtles. Please keep 50 yards away from turtles.

✓ **Open Zone:** Open to activities except for those that could injure coral or live rock or alter the seabed.

Wildlife and Natural Resources in the Park:

STXEEMP was created to protect a wide array of wildlife and natural resources found on St. Croix. The reefs within STXEEMP were created by hard corals such as elkhorn and staghorn corals, as well as various species of brain, lettuce, finger, star and starlet corals. The last half century has seen a significant decline in the quality (health) and quantity (distribution) of these corals in the Caribbean. Although seagrass beds are not as flashy as coral reefs, they are an integral part integral part of the life-cycle of many reef-dwellers. Predatory fish (such as grouper, snapper, shark and barracuda) as well as algae-eating fish (such as parrot fish, doctor fish and surgeon fish) rely on both the reefs and sea grass beds for their food, shelter, and as a breeding ground and nursery. In fact, an estimated 400 species of fish live in and around the East End and utilize these habitats!

Reefs and seagrass beds in the Park's waters are also feeding grounds for hawksbill and green turtles. The beaches along STXEEMP are known nesting grounds for endangered green, hawksbill and leatherback turtles. Over the past few years, populations of green turtles have stabilized, while hawksbill populations are still declining.

In addition to the large variety of marine life, STXEEMP also hosts 17 species of seasonal and year-round nesting seabirds, including: shearwaters, tropicbirds, boobies, pelicans, frigate birds, gulls and terns

Management of the Park and its Resources:

The resources within STXEEMP provide environmental, economic and social benefits to both residents and visitors of St. Croix, so they must be managed in a way that guarantees they remain available for present and future generations. According to The Nature Conservancy, protecting the park is vital because: "Coral reefs are dying because erosion caused by construction sends soils, pollutants and excess nutrients into the Caribbean Sea. The building of houses, restaurants, hotels and other businesses that attract visitors to this tourist-dependent economy is a threat to native plants and animals. Careless divers and boaters harm reefs, and over fishing of species such as grouper, snapper and parrot fish upsets the sea's natural balance and puts the future of fishery stocks in jeopardy. About 70 percent of the U.S. Virgin Islands' original wetlands, prime habitat for nesting seabirds and juvenile fish, have been destroyed. Over-fishing depletes seabirds' food supplies, pollution makes their food unhealthy, and the birds die when they become entangled in fishing gear

DPNR's focus when it comes to STXEEMP is to enhance public understanding of the benefits of the Park, promote responsible recreational use of the park, and to enforce the rules and regulations in order to conserve the natural resources of the park for future generations. DPNR conducts outreach and educational programs, monitoring programs, and is currently working on a new visitor's center and living museum at the STXEEMP office located on the South Shore at Great Pond. To learn more, you can visit the offices of STXEEMP between 8:00am 5:00pm on weekdays or call 340-718-3367.

How You Can Help:

- ✓ Enjoy the STXEEMP responsibly! Follow the park rules and regulations; feel free to call the office with any questions. Keep the shorelines and waters free of trash, and "take nothing but memories, leave nothing but footprints".

- ✓ Support the Friends of St. Croix East End Marine Park organization. There are many ways to get involved!

- ✓ If you witness a suspected violation of the park rules and regulations, call the Park office at 340-718-3367.

- ✓ Volunteer your time on park projects and programs.

Take in the beauty and bounty STXEEMP offers by exploring on your own. You can also learn more about the ecology and history of St.

Croix and the STXEEMP by taking a guided snorkel, kayak tour or bayside tour. However you choose to enjoy STXEEMP, please do so responsibly!

Rainy Day Activities on St. Croix

Many islands in the Caribbean, St. Croix included, are known for their lush, tropical landscape as much as their beautiful beaches. The reason for this gorgeous greenery is the frequently passing rain showers.

Generally speaking, the rain showers come and go quickly, so you just have to find cover for a few minutes and wait them out. During the rainy months however, you are more likely to encounter rainy days and not just passing showers. For those visiting the island, rainy days can dampen your vacation plans; but, if you're flexible, there is still plenty of fun to be had on St. Croix even when it's raining.

Here at GoToStCroix.com we are often asked by visitors: "Is there something I can do or see on St. Croix when it's raining?" The answer is YES! Whether you are travelling alone, enjoying a romantic interlude, or taking the kids on vacation, St. Croix offers something for everyone to do when the rain starts. Here are our picks for the Top 10 Rainy Day Activities:

1. **Go bowling**

We may be a small island, but St. Croix does have a locally owned and operated bowling alley, Tropical Ten Pins Bowling Center. Take your family and friends and hit the lanes for open bowling, great food, and a fun atmosphere. If you happen to be there on a Friday or Saturday night you can enjoy Rave Bowling with great music, a light show, prizes and more!

2. Get a massage or spa treatment

Relax and enjoy the sound of the rain from inside the comfort of one of St. Croix's lovely spas or salons as you indulge in a massage, manicure, pedicure, facial, lash extensions, hair cut or color, or the works. Choose from resort spas, day spas, salons, or even have a massage therapist come to you at your hotel, villa or home!

3. Hit the casino

Enjoy the air conditioned comfort of the Divi Carina Bay Casino as you sip a cocktail, listen to live music, and try your luck at the slots or one of their many table games.

4. Go shopping in downtown Christiansted or Frederiksted

With lots of locally owned shops, galleries, jewelry stores and specialty boutiques located close together along the historic streets you can easily walk between shops, often under awnings or arcades, and do some shopping (or buying!) without getting wet.

5. Eat, drink and be merry

One of my personal favorite ways to enjoy the rain (without being out in it) is to grab a table or bar stool at one of the waterfront restaurants. There you can enjoy a meal, a snack, or even just a cup of coffee or a cocktail as you watch the rain fall on the Caribbean Sea. If you're not close to the waterfront, you can still enjoy many of the island's restaurants while you stay dry and enjoy a delicious meal.

6. Play golf on the indoor simulator

Don't let the rain keep you from playing your 18 holes. The Buccaneer's Pro Shop now offers an indoor golf simulator where you can play on your choice of 93 of the world's best golf courses including Pebble Beach, Torrey Pines, and PGA National. Just call for an appointment!

7. Read a book

It sounds simple, but there is nothing like delving into a good book with the sound of the rain in the background. Even better, head over to Undercover Books & Gifts and peruse their great selection of books and pick out something new. You can even sit outside under the cover of the awning with a coffee and pastry to make your reading even more enjoyable. If you are lucky enough to be there on the right day, they also offer a story hour for kids, readings and book signings.

8. Take an art, fitness or wellness class

The variety and availability of classes is ever expanding on St. Croix, so why not try one out if you need to stay dry? The island offers yoga and fitness classes in several studios and gyms, or get creative at an art class or workshop, you can even find dance lessons occasionally. Your best bet for a variety of classes and workshops is to check with The Courtyard Juices & Fitness Studio or The Blue Mutt.

9. Enjoy some live music or entertainment

Just because it's raining outside doesn't mean the entertainment stops. You can still catch crab races, live music, and even Kiki and the Flaming Gypsies performing at some of the island's popular restaurants, resorts, and even the casino.

10. Watch a movie at the theater

Head to Sunny Isle and take in a newly released movie at the island's only movie theater.

Whether rain or shine, St. Croix offers a variety of fun activities for all. If some of your planned vacation activities get rained out, consider replacing them with an item or two off our *Top 10 Rainy Day Activities* list. Most important of all, keep in mind that the sun will (probably) come out tomorrow, and maybe this rain shower will bring a rainbow!

Have a Beer with Some Pigs

Like many small islands in the Caribbean, St. Croix offers it's own unusual local tourist attractions. Surprisingly, one of our most popular attractions are the beer drinking pigs at the Mt. Pellier Hut Domino Club. Yes, you read correctly! If you stop at the Domino Club, not only can you get yourself a cold beer, but you can buy a round for the resident pigs (non-alcoholic, of course).

Tucked away in the subtropical rainforest of the island's West End, just off of Route 76, is the Mt. Pellier Hut Domino Club. Known to many residents as 'Norma's' after beloved proprietor Norma George, the property houses a small open-air bar and restaurant and a separate out building that is home to stars of the attraction, the beer drinking pigs. For those of you that are animals lovers, rest assured that Norma and the staff of the Domino Club treat the pigs like family pets. They all have names, they are well fed and cared for, and they are never forced to drink (they only get drink the non-alcoholic beer offerings when they want them).

So how did the whole beer-drinking-pig thing get started? Over 25 years ago George and Norma, the farmers that own the place, had decided to downsize the number of pigs they were keeping on the farm. They had sold almost all of their pigs, but decided to keep two as pets: Ms. Piggy and Buster Pig. One day, a visitor of George and Norma's walked passed Buster Pig with a beer in his hand and Buster decided to help himself to a drink! Little did they know that after that day Buster Pig would become a star on the island. As time time went on, people continued to visit George and Norma to have a beer and play some dominoes, and they would give Buster a beer (since he had indicated his love of suds the day he stole his first one). As a result, the Mt. Pellier Hut Domino Club was created and has become one of St. Croix's most well-known and loved attractions

When you get to the Domino Club, head to the bar and order a beer for the pigs. While you're there, do yourself a favor and order one of their house specialties: a shot of the Mama-Wanna (an infused rum made right there on site by Norma herself), or a fresh banana daiquiri. Once you have your O'Doul's for the pig, one of the lovely staff members will take you up to the hut and introduce you to the pigs. Make sure to listen to the instructions before you step up to the pens (don't worry, there aren't many). The fun begins when one of the HUGE pigs jumps up and puts their front legs on the pen door, which means they are ready for a cold one. The pigs will take the whole can of beer right from your hand, chomp on the can with their giant teeth, guzzle the beer, and then spit out the flattened can once they have sucked it dry. They are pigs about it, just as you would imagine!

You have to see this attraction live in person to really get the full effect! Even for those of us that live here, it's still fun to give the pigs a beer and chat with Norma and her friendly staff. If you are visiting the island, you simply must visit the Mt. Pellier Hut Domino Club. Not only is this a budget-friendly attraction, but it doesn't take long, the drive through the rainforest is scenic, and the Domino Club staff will make you feel right at home. Bottoms up...but, don't forget to spit out the can!

Tour Two Historic Forts

Two of the most iconic and imposing historical buildings here on St. Croix are Fort Christiansvaern and Fort Frederik. These forts were constructed between the mid-1700's and mid-1800's to protect Christiansted and Frederiksted from smugglers, pirates, European invaders, as well as to enforce the payment of taxes on imports and exports, and to deter slave rebellions. Both of these forts offer self-guided tours that allow you to step back in time and take in some of the history of St. Croix, or you can take a guided tour with a local guide to enhance your experience.

Alongside Christiansted Harbor, Fort Christiansvaern's yellow walls rise up from the green grass surrounding the Christiansted National Historic Site. Fort Christiansvaern was completed by the Danish in

1749, and was added to from 1835-1841. It's made of Danish yellow bricks and masonry that were imported as ballast in the holds of sailing ships. The structure of the fort itself is a four point citadel surrounding a central courtyard, and it's pastel yellow color is typical of the Danish Colonial style of the era.

Fort Christiansvaern houses an array of original cannons and cannon balls, and features several military exhibits including an arsenal and a furnished Officer's Day Room. You can walk through the dungeon, the latrine, and the courtyard. The fort offers some amazing photo ops with it's striking series of archways, and spectacular views of Christiansted Harbor and the fort itself from the second story. If you are lucky enough to be standing on the second story when historic 138' Roseway schooner sails by you can really get a feel for the history.

In Frederiksted, Fort Frederik's red walls contrast against the beautiful turquoise Caribbean Sea near Frederiksted Pier. This deep red rubble and masonry fort is built in a trapezoidal design that was typical of the classic Danish military architecture of the period. Also known as Frederiksfort, it was built between 1751 and 1760 and named in honor of the reigning Danish monarch, Frederik V. Now a U.S. National Historic Landmark, Fort Frederik Museum houses a furnished commandants quarters, an art gallery with rotating exhibits, and a display about Danish West Indies architectural features. The fort is also home to a very interesting display related to the Fredensborg, a ship that was part of the 'Triangle Trade' of slaves from Europe, to Africa and St. Croix, and back to Europe. The ship sank just off coast in Denmark, but the first mate saved the ship's log. At the fort are records about the sale of the slaves which occurred in St. Croix, as well as a collection of historical items.

Fort Frederik was also was the center of the abolition of slavery in the Virgin Islands as it was here that Danish Governor Peter Von Shoulten emancipated the slaves on July 3, 1848. While the 1848 Emancipation Revolt technically ended slavery in the Danish West Indies, it inaugurated a 30-year period of serfdom based on contract labor that ensured continuing control by plantation owners. Then in 1878, escalating tensions erupted into the Labor Riot and 'Fireburn', which ended the contract labor system.

Whether you choose to take a guided tour, or you choose to use the pamphlets provided by the admissions offices to take a self-guided tour, I recommend touring both of these historic forts. Fort Christiansvaern and Fort Frederik offer different exhibits, different views and photo ops, and they each offer something about the history of St. Croix that is worth exploring. While you could tour each of the forts in about 30-45 minutes, I recommend giving yourself an hour or more so you can read all the historical information provided and take pictures without being rushed. You may also want to plan some extra time to visit the areas around each fort, as both Christiansted and Frederiksted are full of beautiful architecture, local culture, and Crucian history.

Hours and Admission:

Fort Christiansvaern is located at 2100 Church Street in Christiansted, and is open daily from 8:00am to 5:00pm. Admission is $3 per adult, children 16 and under are free with a paid adult. Secure 2 hour parking is available at Fort Christiansvaern until 3:30 pm. To confirm the hours and admission fees, or for additional information, you can call the National Park Service at (340) 773-1460.

Fort Frederik Museum is located at #198 Strand Street in Frederiksted, and is open Monday thru Friday from 8:00am to 4:00pm, and when cruise ships are in port. Admission is $5, children 16 and under are free with a paid adult. Street parking is available along Strand Street, or across the street from the fort. To confirm the hours and admission fees, or for additional information, you can call the Fort Frederik Museum at (340) 772-2021.

Hoist the Sails on a Historic Ship

There are few sights as eye-catching as seeing the Roseway making her way across the turquoise waters of the Caribbean into the harbor. The Roseway is a beautifully restored 137' schooner with massive russet colored sails that is registered as a U.S. National Historic Landmark in both Boston and St. Croix. This regal vessel is owned and operated by the World Ocean School, which operates in the Caribbean from November to April, providing a platform for curriculum integrated educational programs for students of all ages in the islands, and operates out of New England for the remainder of the year. World Ocean School provides programming for low-income pubic school students in both regions.

Roseway was originally designed as a fishing yacht by John James and built in 1925 in his family's shipyard in Essex, Massachusetts. The Roseway is one of only six surviving Grand Banks schooners, and the only schooner specifically designed to beat the Nova Scotians in the international fishing vessel races of the 1920s and 1930s. Following her use for racing and fishing, during World War I in 1942, Roseway was fitted with a .50-caliber machine gun and used by the Boston Pilots Association to guide ships through the minefields and anti-submarine netting protecting the harbor.

After her retirement from naval use in 1973, Roseway was transformed into a Windjammer and started cruising in 1975. Roseway then starred in the television remake of Rudyard Kipling's

'Captains Courageous' in 1977. Finally, in September 2002, the bank that owned the Roseway honored a request by the World Ocean School and donated Roseway to be used for the school. Since then, St. Croix has become the winter home port for Roseway and she summers in the Northeast, primarily in Boston, providing educational programs and day sails for the public.

I highly recommend that you book a day sail on the Roseway while here on St. Croix and allow yourself the amazing experience of hoisting the sails on this historic tall-ship! Stepping onto the ship is like stepping back in time. As you stand on the wooden deck make sure to look up and marvel at the enormity of the two masts. Also, make sure to tour the entire deck and take in the details of this impressive schooner such as the intricate rigging, the wooden helm, the huge anchor stowed on the port side of the bow, the beautiful brass ships bell, and the array of knots used for both utility and stowage of the lines.

Once underway, you will be given the opportunity to be part of the action as the crew recruits passengers to grab a line and help to hoist the 5,600 square feet of sails. After lining up along the side of the ship, you firmly plant your feet and grasp the huge line in your hand, then the staff crew leads as you rhythmically hoist the sail by pulling the line hand-over-hand in unison (or heave, ho as the sailors say). The weight of the sails is unbelievable, and it feels very rewarding to look up at the billowing sails and know that you were part of the 'crew' that raised them up those massive masts.

Once the sails are up, enjoy the smooth sailing Roseway offers here around St. Croix as you relax on deck and enjoy the view, or explore the vessel and take in the splendor of this sailing landmark. The Roseway is docked on St. Croix from November through April, and offers sunset sails to the public Sunday Friday, as well as public day sails and private charters. To book your sail, or to confirm the current schedule and cost, please call (340) 626-7877 or visit www.roseway.com. Come and be part of history today by hoisting the sails and experiencing the National Historic Landmark that is the Roseway

Visit the Site of Colombus' Landing

Salt River Bay National Historic Park and Ecological Preserve on St. Croix contains the only known site where members of an expedition led by Christopher Columbus set foot on what is now United States territory.

In 1493, on his second visit to the New World, Christopher Columbus sent a party of men ashore to the area now known as Columbus Landing. You can visit the spot where this historical event took place and learn about the Columbus expedition landing, the native Carib and Taino tribes, and much more at the Salt River Bay Visitor's Center.

The last of the native people to inhabit St. Croix were the Carib. Originally from the Guiana region of South America, the Carib people had gained presence of the islands from the Tainos (or Arawaks) in the early 1400's. It was, however, the Carib that greeted Columbus on his second voyage through the islands. On that fateful day of November 14, 1493, Columbus sent a landing party of about two dozen men ashore to St. Croix, which he had named Santa Cruz (or 'Holy Cross'). Upon entering a deserted Carib village, the Spanish found a small group of Taino captives who agreed to accompany them back to their ship. While returning to their ship, the Spanish encountered a Carib war party. In the ensuing fight one of Columbus' men was wounded by an arrow; he died several days later. This altercation was the first documented conflict between Europeans and Native Americans.

Over 600 years later, Salt River Bay National Historic Park and Ecological Preserve is a blend of history, sea, and land that holds some of the largest remaining mangrove forests in the Virgin Islands, as well as coral reefs and a submarine canyon. This area has been witness to thousands of years of human endeavor and every major period of human habitation in the Virgin Islands is represented, from several

South American Indian cultures to attempts at colonization by a succession of European nations, along with enslaved West Africans and their descendants. The area around Salt River contains the remains of some 1,500 years of Saladoid (Igneri), Ostinoid, Taino, and Carib occupation. During the Taino occupation, the area served as the seat of a chiefdom, which contained an important religious structure, and a ball and dance court. Over 100 years of archeological investigations have demonstrated that the Salt River Bay area was the focus of the most extensive and intensive prehistoric occupation in the U.S. Virgin Islands.

The Columbus Landing Site was designated a National Historic Landmark on October 9, 1960, and on February 24, 1992 Congress created the Salt River Bay National Historic Park and Ecological Preserve, under cooperative management of the National Park Service (NPS) and Government of the Virgin Islands of the United States. As a historic area of the NPS, the park was administratively listed on the National Register of Historic Places on the same day. You can learn more about the fascinating history of Salt River Bay, including Columbus' landing, at the Visitor Center. The Visitor Center is open November 14 through June each year on Tuesdays and Thursdays from 9:30 AM until 4:00 PM, so please plan your trip accordingly. When the Visitor Center is closed, information about Salt River Bay may be obtained at the National Park Service visitor contact station at Fort Christianvaern, Christiansted National Historic Site between the hours of 8:30 AM and 4:30 PM daily.

Drive to Point Udall, Easternmost Point of the U.S

While you are here on St. Croix, I recommend that you take the very scenic drive all the way up to Point Udall at the far East End of the island. Point Udall offers stunning panoramic sea views, and is the easternmost point of the United States. Home to the Millennium Monument, this tranquil point is must on any St. Croix 'to do' list.

As you drive the winding road that leads to Point Udall, you will see that the arid climate on the East End of St. Croix hosts a variety of cactus and desert-like foliage in stark contrast to the turquoise waters of the Caribbean. You can look up towards the south and see Goat Hill rising above the road, and you can look out across the Caribbean Sea to Buck Island to the north. As you reach Point Udall, named for former Secretary of the Interior, Stuart Udall, the Millennium Monument comes into view right in front of you.

The Millennium Monument was designed by Bill Rich and erected in 2000 to commemorate the beginning of a new millennium for the United States. The monument is a giant sundial which is fitting since Point Udall is the first place the sun rises on U.S. soil. In fact, special ceremonies were held at Point Udall as the sun rose on the most easternmost of American soils in the western hemisphere on the first day of the new millennium, January 1, 2000. There is a huge sign denoting Point Udall on the retaining wall at the base of the monument that makes for a great photo op, so don't miss it!

Once you have perused the monument, make sure to take in the surrounding view, because it is truly breathtaking. Looking down below you to the east and south, you will be captivated by the multi-blue, reef-laden waters and the waves crashing on the shore. To the northwest you will see Buck Island off in the distance. Enjoy the peace and quiet Point Udall offers, with only the sounds of the crashing waves and wind, and the occasional murmur of other visitors.

There is no admission charge to visit Point Udall and the Millennium Monument, so spend as much or as little time as you would like. If you would like to make a day of it, you can hike down to Jack's and Isaac's Bays from the small parking lot just below the monument for some great snorkeling. Of course, one of the most popular times to visit Point Udall is at sunrise. If you do go first thing in the morning, you can also hike up to the top of Goat Hill for an amazing view of St. Croix.

As is always a good rule of thumb in any tourist area, we recommend that you do not leave valuables in your car. Also, be advised that there is no cell phone reception on the far East End of the island, and there are no stores nearby. We recommend that you bring plenty of water, snacks, sun protection, and your snorkel gear if you want to head down to Jack's and Isaac's. Maybe consider taking a picnic breakfast or lunch with you and spend some time taking in the tranquility of Point Udall while you dine alfresco. Whatever you choose to do when you arrive, enjoy the incredibly scenic drive to Point Udall, the easternmost point of the U.S.!

Reconnect with Nature at the Botanical Garden

The nature and history of St. Croix come together in perfect harmony at the St. George Village Botanical Garden. This sprawling sixteen acre property is a quiet haven of beautiful foliage mingled with rambling historic plantation ruins.

Come reconnect with nature, relax amongst the shade trees, and take in the delicate fragrances and diverse scenery the gardens provide.

For nature lovers and horticulturists, the botanical garden has a collection with over 1,000 native and exotic species and varieties including a medicinal herb garden, an orchid house, a trail through rainforest, a fruit orchard, a cactus garden, a palm garden, and much, MUCH more. The plants are labeled with little black and white signs, so along the way you can learn the name, native location, description and uses of the plants. When you check in at the Visitors' Center Gift Shop, you will receive a detailed self-guided tour map that will lead you through the botanical splendor and historical structures the garden offers.

As you meander along the shaded pathways you will see massive native trees (including Kapok, Mahogany, and Turpentine), vining plants with huge leaves, lush ferns, a rainbow of colorful flowers, dripping Spanish moss, and tropical fruit trees. In addition to the flora the garden offers, it is home to a variety of local fauna as well. Keep an eye out for bananaquits (the official bird of the U.S. Virgin Islands), hummingbirds, butterflies, lizards, hard-working bees, mongoose, and dragonflies

For those who appreciate history, St. George Village Botanical Garden is dotted with both restored buildings and preserved ruins of the Estate St. George Danish sugar plantation, originally built in the 18th and 19th century. Several gardens are now located in the Sugar and Rum Factory ruins, and the Overseer's House is currently home to a group of Jamaican fruit bats. The Blacksmith Shop, including many of it's tools and furnishings, has been preserved and is still in use. The Workers' Family Quarters buildings now house the St. George Village Museum, the Library, and the Orchid House. Around the The Manager's House you will find the garden's Herbarium collection of over 5,000 dried and pressed plant specimens, which represent about

80% of the plant species known to be growing in the U.S. Virgin Islands and are very important for research and historical purposes

Estate St. George also overlaps an Amerindian settlement which dates back to 100 A.D. The Amerindian settlers made their way up the Caribbean islands from the Saladero region in what is now Venezuela. These skilled horticulturists had already been cultivating cassava for centuries and the Saladoid culture (and later groups) carried many crops with them from South America through the islands, such as hot peppers, sweet potatoes, peanuts, and pineapples. It is likely that the Amerindians chose the Estate St. George site because the fresh water stream that is now Mint Gut would have given them access to the South Shore of the island via canoe. The Saladoid inhabitants occupied the area until about 1,000 A.D. when they apparently dispersed to other island locations.

If you are a photographer (professional, amateur, or otherwise) you will find the garden truly inspirational! Aside from the overwhelming amount flora and fauna, there are great photo ops at the Japanese Bridge, the gardens in the Sugar and Rum Factory ruins, and at the towering Kapok tree in front of the Great Hall. So, charge up that camera battery!

The St. George Village Botanical Garden also offers many great educational programs, activities and events throughout the year. For kids, they host a 'Story Hour in the Garden' under the Kapok tree, as well as a series of 'Second Saturday' workshops for children and their parents to learn together. The garden also offers a series of 'Grow & Learn' workshops for adults, and a twice-monthly 'Lunch in Garden' featuring a three course meal prepared by students from the St. Croix Career and Technical Education Center (CTEC). The garden also hosts annual events such as Art in the Garden, Eco-Fair, Mango Melee, and Christmas Spoken Here. For specific dates and times currently available for the garden's activities, workshops and events

In my opinion, no trip to St. Croix is complete without a visit to the St. George Village Botanical Garden! In about an hours time you learn about St. Croix's plant life, see some historical ruins and preserved plantation buildings, and commune with nature. Please keep in mind that the garden is a non-profit organization, so your admission supports the garden and its programs directly. If you enjoy your visit to the garden and find you would like to do more, you can become a member, volunteer, give a donation

Scuba Diving

Dive into the beautiful turquoise waters of the Caribbean to see a stunning and unique underwater world only St. Croix has to offer. In addition to sea turtles and reef sharks, the thousands of tropical reef fish of the Caribbean are colourful and diverse. From the underwater canyons of Salt River, to the The Wall of the Puerto Rico Trench off Cane Bay, the topography offers something for every scuba diver. St. Croix even has a few wrecks and a carousel horse! The Frederiksted Pier is a not-to-be-missed dive that is abundant with seahorses, puffer fish and octopus, and it makes an amazing night dive! There are dive shops located all over the island to meet all your diving needs from boat trips to gear rentals and sales. You can even use your time underwater to advance your dive certifications. Happy diving!

Dive the Salt River Canyon Sites

In the Caribbean Sea, just outside of St. Croix's Salt River Bay, can be found a breathtaking underwater geographical feature known as the Salt River Canyon. This underwater canyon is formed by the remains of an ancient river and waterfall that formed a deep "V" in the wall of the Puerto Rico Trench that runs just off of the island's North Shore. As you can imagine, diving the canyon is like stepping back in time. You can almost visualize the prehistoric river and waterfall running as you look across the geographical features still present under the surface of the sea today, thousands of years later, now teeming with fish, coral, sponges, and sea fans.

Not only is it a unique place to dive, but Salt River Canyon is an extremely historical site as well. Christopher Columbus came to this site on his second trip to American, bringing 17 ships with him. Unfortunately, there was bloodshed between the native Caribs and the Spanish, and Columbus took some of the Tiano captives from the Carib village back to Europe with him. On a happier note, the canyon is also one of the oldest geological areas in the Caribbean. This historic area was also home to the Aquarius Hydrolab, a NOAA Underwater Research Centre, in the 1970's and 80's. The Aquarius Hydrolab allowed scientists to live underwater for a week or so at a time doing research on the geology, corals, and fish life in the canyon. The Wall itself brings a rich biodiversity of life due to the mixing of nutrients where the deep waters of the Puerto Rico Trench meet the shallow reefs, making the canyon was the perfect place for Aquarius Hydrolab to be housed.

As a diver on St. Croix, don't miss out on seeing the beauty and magnitude of the Salt River Canyon for yourself. The *U.S. Virgin Islands Top 10 Dive Sites* article in *Scuba Diving* magazine described Salt River Canyon well when they wrote: "St. Croix's north shore is one of the best-kept secrets in wall diving, and this site has two walls facing each other across a quarter mile of blue water. Hordes of reef fish swarm the tops of the walls, deep-water sea fans and black coral cling to the deeper sections, and big animals like hammerheads and black-tips sometimes make appearances." While it is true that the East Wall and West Wall of the canyon are only a quarter of a mile apart, they offer two very different diving experiences. I highly recommend doing both!

Salt River Canyon's East Wall has a mooring which lies in about 40 feet of water. However, due to the vertical drop of The Wall in this location, when moored the back of the dive boats often hang over a depth of 1,000 feet! Often referred to as "the fishiest dive on the North Shore", the East Wall of the canyon boasts tons of reef fish at the top of The Wall. From about 40-80 feet, The Wall slopes down into sand chutes between large formations of hard corals, covered with sponges and soft corals.

This area boasts huge schools of black durgeon, yellowtail snapper, soldier fish and striped grunts. At around 80 feet The Wall drops off into the blue abyss and you will often see black tip reef sharks and large spotted eagle rays. Thanks to the gradual slope before the drop-off, the East Wall is also home to numerous tropical species in addition to pelagic species, including moray eels, large numbers of barracuda (hence the dive site name 'Barracuda Bank'), large angel fish, parrot fish, lobster and conch. Hammerhead sharks have even been spotted lurking off the East Wall.

Salt River Canyon's West Wall has a mooring in just 20 feet of water, but is a sheer drop to 200 feet, then 500 feet, and then down The Wall to 4,000 foot depths. This portion of the canyon is known as 'The Pinnacles' due to the geological formations believed to have been formed by an ancient, above ground waterfall. These formations offer a maze of swim-throughs, cuts, ledges, overhangs, recesses and sand chutes to be explored. At this site you will likely see rays gliding around 'The Pinnacles', while schools of creole wrasse, black durgeon, and squirrelfish can be found under ledges and swimming off the edge of the wall. As you descend, you will find jacks, grouper, permits, barracudas, as well as large pelagic sea life such as sharks. While there is a seeming endless amount of fish to see, don't overlook the geological features of the canyon itself. There are few dive sites in the world that offer the unique features you can find here on the West Wall. In fact, the West Wall of Salt River Canyon is the most requested boat dive on St. Croix.

When diving the canyon, you may also see diver favorites such as sea turtles, spotted eagle rays, and dolphins. If you are lucky enough to be here in February or March, you may even be serenaded by the humpback whales' song as they migrate along the Puerto Rio Trench. Among the crags and corals you may also find historical ship anchors dating from the 1700-1800's. In Salt River Canyon and along The Wall, history, geology, and biology mix to form some of the most unique and diverse dive sites in the world. While there are many amazing dive sites the island offers, please make sure to dive the Salt River Canyon. St. Croix is home to several world-class dive operators that show you the canyon sites and the underwater beauty they behold.

Advance Your Scuba Diving Skills on St. Croix

St. Croix is known in the scuba community for the amazing diving to be found here. Divers travel from all over the world to dive The Wall, Cane Bay, Salt River Canyon and the Frederiksted Pier.

In addition to offering some well recognized dive sites, St. Croix offers warm Caribbean water, great visibility, and an abundance of diverse marine life. The combination of great dive conditions, coupled with the variety of PADI professional dive shops on the island, make St. Croix a great location for divers to advance their skills.

If you come to St. Croix as a recreational Open Water Diver, you will have a wonderful dive experience. But, while you are here in paradise, why not take the opportunity to advance your dive skills as well? If you are a relatively new diver, consider earning your Advance Open Water certification. Advance Open Water is a great way to build your diving confidence and expand your scuba skills through different kinds of 'Adventure Dives' such as deep diving, underwater navigation, night diving, buoyancy control, fish identification, wreck diving, photography, and more. If you want to stay down longer and get back in the water sooner on repetitive dives, earn your Enriched Air Diver certification since enriched air nitrox gives you more no decompression time.

St. Croix offers a variety of dive experiences, so you may want to earn some PADI Specialty certifications that will enrich your underwater experience on St. Croix. The Frederiksted Pier is a world renowned night dive, so that would be a great location to earn your Night Diver specialty. Butler Bay houses five different wrecks, both shallow and deep, as well as remnants of the old NOAA HydroLab. The three shallow wrecks are a great location to earn a Wreck Diver specialty. If you have always imagined taking pictures of the amazing sea life you encounter on your dives, The Wall and Frederiksted Pier offer amazing photo ops making them perfect to earn a Digital Underwater Photographer specialty.

For some advanced divers, St. Croix is an ideal setting to work on more professional level certifications. Tech Diving is popular here on the island due to the depth of the Puerto Rico Trench and The Wall it creates. Many of the local dive shops also offer Divemaster and

Instructor certifications, so if you are considering a possible career in scuba St. Croix is a great place to get started.

Scuba diving opens up a whole new world of adventures and opportunities. In fact, *Scuba Diving* magazine's readers named the U.S. Virgin Islands in the Top 5 for Places in the Caribbean and Atlantic for: Best Dive Destination, Wall Diving, Underwater Photography, Beginner Diving and more. If you are going to advance your dive skills, St. Croix offers friendly and professional dive shops that will help you earn your new certification while having a once in a lifetime dive experience. You can even start your learning and classroom work online before coming to St. Croix, so you can spend more time in the water! Visit the links below to find the right dive shop for you, and to learn more about diving on St. Croix. See you down there!

Dive the World Famous Cane Bay Wall

St. Croix is known for world class Caribbean diving. Beneath the turquoise waters the island is almost completely surrounded by a barrier reef teeming with coral, sponges, schools of tropical fish, sea turtles, and more. The most well-known part of this spectacular coral reef runs along the North Shore of St. Croix and is known simply as 'The Wall'.

The Wall is created by the Puerto Rico trench located on the boundary between the Caribbean Sea and the Atlantic Ocean. The trench itself is

497 miles long and at its deepest point, known as Milwaukee Deep (located 76 miles north of Puerto Rico), it has a depth of at least 28,373 feet! For divers, the depth of the Puerto Rico Trench off St. Croix (about 3,200 feet) makes it a great site for deep diving, tech diving, and regular recreational diving. Even better, it can be accessed by shore or by boat at numerous dive sites along the North Shore of the island.

The most popular site for shore diving this amazing feature is the Cane Bay Wall located just off Cane Bay Beach. Many divers, myself included, surface swim the 200+ yards from the boat ramp on Cane Bay Beach out to the white mooring buoy before descending. While you can descend earlier and swim out, surface swimming to the buoy allows you to spend more time on Cane Bay Wall. I recommend that you take your time making the surface swim as there can be swells and surge in Cane Bay at times, and it is a 200 yard swim...trust me, you don't want to exhaust yourself before you even start your dive.

When you descend at the buoy, you drop down to 30-40 feet, then swim between large coral reef structures along a sand chute (known as 3 Anchor Chute) to The Wall. When you first descend, keep an eye out for the famous 'seahorse'. This is a great photo op if you are an underwater photographer. As you swim along 3 Anchor Chute you will want to watch for turtles, stingrays, peacock flounder, and lobster, as well as barrel sponges and sea fans.

When you reach Cane Bay Wall, make sure to look all around you and take in the magnitude of this natural wonder. On one side you will see colorful reef fish of all shapes and sizes, among the coral you will find eels, shrimp, and occasionally, a nurse shark. On the other side of you lies the open ocean. Don't forget to look out towards the blue abyss as you swim along Cane Bay Wall as you will often see reef sharks or barracuda, and occasionally dolphins. If you are really lucky, you may see (or hear) humpback whales as they migrate through the Puerto Rico Trench.

When heading back towards shore to make your ascent, take your time as you swim along the soft coral beds and sand; you may find a real seahorse, jawfish, flamingo tongues, sea turtles, spotted eagle rays, or conch. There is also a coral restoration garden at the orange buoy to the north of the 'seahorse' that is worth a look if your bottom time and air consumption are good.

Cane Bay Wall offers something great for every level of diver. The barrier reef and The Wall are both an underwater photographer and a fish identification enthusiast's dream come true. Any of St. Croix's friendly dive shops can take you out to dive The Wall by boat, or you can rent gear, tanks, and weights right across the street from Cane Bay Beach at the Cane Bay Dive Shop. Whichever you choose, have a safe and memorable dive...maybe I'll see you down there!

Discover Scuba Diving!

Have you ever wanted to try scuba diving so you could see the underwater world up close? It is a whole different world below the surface, and it is truly amazing! If you want to try scuba diving, but you aren't quite ready to take the plunge into full certification, then Discover Scuba is a great option for you. Discover Scuba Diving will allow you to swim with the throngs of tropical fish along St. Croix's colorful reefs under the supervision of a instructor after just an hour or so of training.

There are several dive shops here on St. Croix that offer the PADI (Professional Association of Diving Instructors) Discover Scuba Diving program. The PADI instructors and dive shop staff here on St. Croix are very friendly and professional. Even better, they are experienced and calm which will make your Discover Scuba experience relaxed and incredibly fun. Not only will you have an opportunity to feel the thrill that comes with descending down to the reefs and exploring their abundant marine life, but you experience the excitement that comes with breathing underwater.

What can you expect from a Discover Scuba Diving experience? To start, you will spend 1-2 hours learning basic scuba diving skills in a swimming pool, or in calm, shallow water. Once you are comfortable with the necessary skills, you get to go out and dive one of St. Croix's stunning reefs with your PADI Instructor by your side. While you will not obtain a scuba certification, the Discover Scuba Diving experience is a quick and easy introduction to the knowledge, basic skills, and equipment needed to explore the underwater world. No prior scuba diving experience is necessary to sign up for a Discover Scuba Diving program, but you must be at least 10 years old and you need to be in reasonable physical health.

St. Croix is one of the best places I can imagine for doing a Discover Scuba. Why? For starters, the water temperature in this part of the Caribbean stays between 80°F and 82°F year round, which is warm and pleasant for divers. Visibility is also very good around St. Croix most of the year, generally ranging from 60-100 feet. What does that mean to you as a Discover Scuba diver? While you are exploring the underwater world, you will be able to look up and see the surface of the water as well as the sunlight streaming down and reflecting off the white sandy bottom. The clear visibility and good light generally found on St. Croix make it easier to spot some of the hundreds of species of fish that camouflage themselves on or around the reefs and sand, or hide under the coral heads. Keep an eye out for sea turtles, seahorses, flounder, frog fish, lizard fish, eels, reef sharks, shrimp, octopus, reef squid, and innumerable tropical fish, all of which are relatively common on St. Croix.

In my opinion, one of the most relaxing things about scuba diving is that you will hear very little besides the rhythmic sound of your own breathing but don't worry, you will be able to communicate with your instructor using basic hand signals, or a slate. You will hover over the bottom, seemingly weightless, and feel like you are part of the marine environment. As you make your way along the reef, make sure to look around you and take everything in. While the reef will be teeming with life, sea turtles, sharks, barracuda, and more can be seen in the open ocean as well. Also, make sure to keep an eye on your instructor because they will know how and where to find an array of sea creatures to show you during your dive.

Deep Diving on St. Croix with S.C.U.B.A.

Divers in the know are already aware that St. Croix boasts some of the best diving in the Caribbean, and the best (by far) in the Virgin Islands. With our diverse combination of wrecks, reefs and walls, there is no shortage of dive sites on St. Croix. Most are accessible by a short boat ride since the barrier reefs hug the shoreline so snugly. The north shore has a canyon wall that drops almost 13,200 feet and at certain access points like Cane Bay, is just a quick and easy swim from the beach. But unless you are properly trained to dive deeper than recreational dive limits allow, you may never see what's 'really' down there. St. Croix Ultimate Bluewater Adventures (S.C.U.B.A.) wants to change all that by introducing PADI TecRec to the Virgin Islands, exclusively available on St. Croix. This may make your St. Croix dive experience go from incredible to simply mind-blowing.

That's where Captain Jon Kieren and Instructor Lauren Fanning come in. This dynamic couple is passionate about the incredible diving on St. Croix, and are trained professionals in the sport of Technical Diving. With more than 3000 Open-Water Dives under their collective belts, and more than 200 Tec Dives, John and Lauren have (pardon the cliche) "Boldly gone where few men have gone before". They have explored caves at 270 feet on the North Shore's popular dive spot named Northstar. At Salt River Canyon, they found an enormous anchor which became part of an important survey. Heck, they even got engaged at 350 feet under water - that is 9 atmospheres down!

When I asked Lauren and Jon what they love about Tec Diving, the answer surprised me. Besides the obvious reasons (beautiful and plentiful marine life, some rare species, peacefulness), the response was: "It is a mental exercise above everything else. You cannot panic and quickly surface when you are that deep, which forces you to be completely focused in the moment and be at one with the equipment and environment." When she surfaces from a deep dive, Lauren feels cleansed and liberated, an empowering experience.

For the elite diver who wants to go deeper and stay longer, Tec Diving requires advance certifications such as deep water, nitrox and rescue. S.C.U.B.A. has a series of courses (and will work with your schedule) to properly train divers on safety, equipment, and even a "Trimix Diver" course, which uses a blend of Oxygen, Nitrogen and Helium gasses that permit a diver to safely dive to 210 feet. Lauren is also a "Sidemount Instructor" and can offer you training with the latest dive gear that allows two smaller tanks to be worn on the sides of the body - below shoulders and along the hips - instead of the more standard back mounted tank, which can be tough on a bad back.

Tec Diving is a commitment one must be willing to make. It is an investment of time, money, discipline and mental fortitude. While not for everyone, those who do it will have a view of the world seldom seen by other humans. If this interests you, consider a dive vacation to St. Croix. You can schedule an intensive extended stay and immerse yourself in training, or complete the certification in stages over time. The staff at S.C.U.B.A. is friendly, knowledgable and professional, and passionate about their work. The equipment is top quality and well maintained, and the experience will change your life!

Location : Christiansted

Phone : (877) 567-1367 | (340) 773-5994

Website : www.stcroixscuba.com

The Friendliest Dive Shop on Earth! Let SCUBA's team of Dive Professionals show you why they were rated in the TOP 10 in the Caribbean/Atlantic and why their customers call them 'The Friendliest Dive Shop on Earth'. Visit SCUBA to try diving for the first time, get certified, or become a better diver while witnessing the largest living reef of any Caribbean Island. SCUBA also has a large selection of T-shirts, swimsuits, and Scuba Pro dive/snorkel gear in the Scuboutique

Shop Local

The island of St. Croix offers some amazing locally made products. Both locals and visitors enjoy shopping for beautiful handcrafted jewelry made made in precious metals by local artisans. But, St. Croix also offers locally distilled rum, homemade spice blends and teas, local honey, and a myriad of handmade bath and body products. Find books written by resident authors at our local bookstores and vendor booths, and peruse a wide range of local art in galleries, studios and shops. Whatever your heart desires, you can find souvenirs and goods handmade made right here on our beautiful island. Thank you for supporting St. Croix's island community by shopping for locally made products.

St. Croix Fashion February

St. Croix is full of talented artists, designers, jewelers, and craftspeople. While many annual events are designed to showcase local artisans, those in the fashion industry tend to be overlooked...but, that's about to change! The local fashion community is collaborating to begin an annual event they call "Fashion February". Fashion February will promote local fashion businesses while highlighting the services offered by their non-profit partner, the Women's Coalition of St. Croix. The main event will the Crucian Fashion Fest show, which will bring all of the participants together to showcase just how much fashion talent St. Croix has to offer.

Like the Taste of St. Croix event does for the culinary community, Fashion February will spotlight the businesses that lead the ever-growing fashion industry here on St. Croix. According to Lori Hirons, designer and owner of Island Contessa, and the organizer of the event: "The idea is to celebrate members of the fashion community on St. Croix designers, boutiques, everyone that works to promote the industry on our amazing rock." What started out last year as a small fashion show in a restaurant courtyard with only two participating businesses, has blossomed into a much larger event this year, and the hope is that the event will continue to grow steadily each year.

This year's Fashion February will culminate on on Sunday, February 26th, when eleven of the island's designers, boutique owners, stylists, and jewelers will come together for the inaugural Crucian Fashion Fest. This fashion show will be held in the beautiful open-air lobby of the newly renovated Caravelle Hotel & Casino, where 8-10 models will showcase clothing, accessories, and stylings from the participating businesses. The models will be representatives from the Women's Coalition of St. Croix, and 100% of the ticket sales for this event will be donated to the Women's Coalition.

Tickets for this event are available for purchase at the participating stores, as well as at the Women's Coalition office. Those businesses participating in this year's event are: Adorn, Crucian Gold, Cueros, Envii Boutique, Hotheads, ib designs, Island Contessa, Joyia Jewelry, Molly's, The Boardwalk Parlour and Susan Mango. Two tiers of tickets are available: $10 will get you a General Admission ticket to the show; or, $35 will get you a VIP ticket which includes a reserved seat, a glass of champagne, and a swag bag. VIP seating is limited, so get your tickets today!

The hope of the island's fashion community is that Fashion February will eventually become a series of events similar to New York Fashion Week, attended not only by the local community, but also by off-island visitors, buyers, media, and fashionistas from around the world. St. Croix may be a small island, but we have a lot of fashion talent to share with the Caribbean and the world. Don't miss your chance to get in on the ground floor and enjoy Fashion February's Crucian Fashion Fest while it is still an intimate, community event

Pop-Ups on St. Croix

The "pop-up" revolution is happening across the globe, and the island of St. Croix is embracing the concept. What is a "pop-up"? A pop-up is basically a temporary venue for a business. From retailers to restaurants, the pop-up trend involves a business "popping up" one day, then disappearing the next day (or even weeks later).

Small business and online retailers are finding pop-ups to be a great way to get the word out about their products and services, and those of us consumers that attend the pop-ups are enjoying a fun and unique experience.

Here on St. Croix, the most popular pop-up shops tend to occur during Art Thursdays, since hundreds of people come out to tour Christiansted's galleries and shops. Artists, photographers, jewelers and designers rent out open retail spaces during this time to showcase and sell their products. Often times several business owners will pool their resources to rent a large space to share, creating a sort of indoor mini-mall. Pop-ups are really fun places to shop! Not only do you get to see, feel and experience products that you might not otherwise, but many pop-ups will offer special deals, raffle prizes, or coupons. Pop-ups are also great venues for businesses to unveil new products, or clear out old ones at discounted prices. As a consumer shopping at a pop-up you often have the opportunity to meet and chat with the owner of the business, and/or the artist. Plus, pop-ups are a great way for you to shop local and support St. Croix based businesses!

As for caterers and chefs, pop-up restaurants offer a venue for them to demonstrate their culinary skills and let the public sample their food if only for a night or two. Most often, pop-up restaurants here on St. Croix are held at existing restaurants during their off hours. The beauty of pop-up restaurants is the unlimited types of cuisine that can be offered, and the ambiance that can be created, even for just one evening. Anything goes! For instance, I recently enjoyed a three course French dinner on Bastille Day at a pop-up restaurant. Umami Catering utilized The Bistro's indoor and outdoor spaces and created a French-style cafe for the evening. It was a great evening in a unique setting that featured delicious food prepared by a local chef that does not have a brick-and-mortar restaurant right now.

For business owners there are various benefits to pop-ups such as marketing online businesses, or testing products, locations, or markets. The pop-up concept also allows online businesses to showcase their goods or services and drive traffic to their website. Some pop-up shops are seasonal, which is perfect for those businesses looking to capture foot traffic without committing to a long-term lease. Pop-ups are also a beneficial thing for the landowners because they showcase the store front or restaurant spaces that would otherwise be sitting empty, possibly leading to their use for future pop-ups or even for a long term lease.

Here on St. Croix, pop-ups are a great way for you to enjoy a unique and exclusive experience while supporting local businesses. Check our Calendar of Events for any upcoming pop-up shops or restaurants that we know about, and make sure to keep an eye out you never know what will be popping up next!

Clean Silver Jewelry in Five Easy Ways

We love our handmade jewelry here on St. Croix! If you look around you will find most women wearing stacks of bracelets, not to mention rings, earrings, and necklaces. But, it's not just the women, the men of St. Croix sport their locally crafted jewelry as well. Artisan handmade jewelry is a trademark of the island, and while you can find jewelry crafted from every kind of precious metal, sterling silver is the most common. Silver jewelry can be hard to keep clean, so I was thrilled to find a blog written by ib designs that outlined 5 easy ways to clean your silver jewelry. Here's what they have to say...

Sterling silver reacts to differing pH levels of your personal body chemistry. You must take care not to expose your sterling or 14kt jewelry to chlorine, bleaching agents or chemicals. Your jewelry can always be cleaned with your polishing cloth, but if a deeper cleaning is needed use one of the methods below.

1. Alka-Seltzer: Let tarnished silver sit for a couple of minutes in a glass of fizzing Alka-Seltzer.

2. Aluminum Foil: Line a small bowl with the foil, fill the bowl with hot water, and mix in 1 tbsp non-bleach powdered laundry detergent. Let silver soak for a just a minute. The chemical reaction with the foil will clean it.

3. Ammonia: Soak silver for 10 minutes in a solution of 1/2 cup ammonia and 1/2 cup warm water. Use an old toothbrush to scrub your pieces, then rinse with water.

4. Vinegar: Soak silver for 2-3 hours in a mixture of 4 cups white vinegar and 1 cup baking soda.

5. Ketchup: A silver ring or bracelet can be cleaned by dunking it in a small bowl of ketchup for a few minutes.

With each of these methods you can use an old toothbrush to get in the crevices, then rinse with water, and use your polishing cloth. You can also bring in or send your jewelry to us for special ib love and have your piece look like new for $4.

- Written by ib designs (introduction by Jennie Ogden, Editor)

Thank you to ib designs for sharing these tips for making our silver jewelry shine like new!

Location : Christiansted

Phone : (340) 773-4322

Website : www.islandboydesigns.com

Handcrafted Feel Good Jewelry! This wondrous gallery in historic Christiansted is home to the distinctive designs of local artist/metalsmith, Whealan Massicott and his talented artisan family. Whealan is motivated by the complexity of the Caribbean's people, beauty, and culture. Being a musician at heart allows life's movements, patterns, and rhythms to play out in his raw, organic designs. Whealan's richness of imagination, his creativity, and his material invention allows each piece to express diversity, emotion, and the natural beauty of life. Our Infinity, Gratitude, Strength, and Karma collections are sure to make you FEEL GOOD! Please stop in and say hi

Find the Perfect St. Croix Keepsake

While many would agree that St. Croix is a pretty unforgettable place, most who travel here will leave with some sort of souvenir to remind them of their time on the island. From shot glasses and coffee mugs, to t-shirts and picture frames, everyone tends to collect something different as mementos of their travels. If you are looking for the perfect St. Croix keepsake, visit Purple Papaya for the island's largest selection of souvenirs.

If you want to wear your keepsake, Purple Papaya offers a huge selection of St. Croix t-shirts and apparel for men, women and children. Choose from hundreds of different printed t-shirts, or have one custom made right there in the store. In addition to their t-shirts, you can find embroidered polo shirts, tropical button-downs and shorts for men, and dresses and cover-ups for women. For the kids you can find dresses, rompers, onesies, and even 'magic' color-changing t-shirts. You can also find a variety of accessories, including jewelry and hats in all shapes, sizes and colors.

Shot glasses have always been a popular keepsake and gift, probably because they are small and easy to pack (not to mention useful). Purple Papaya offers a large assortment of shot glasses with fun Caribbean sayings and themes, so you're sure to find just the right one. Don't forget the rum! If you can't decide what flavor of locally made Cruzan Rum to buy, get a variety pack! Purple Papaya offers a great variety sampler pack, or you can belly-up to their Cruzan Rum tasting bar and taste a few samples right in the store. For those non-drinkers, pick up a St. Croix coffee mug to remind you of the island when you are back home sipping your morning cup of joe.

While your memories of St. Croix will last a lifetime, why not frame a picture of a special vacation moment? Purple Papaya offers some fun island-style frames and photo albums, so you can just display a photo from your trip that captured your favorite moment or memory. If you're not one for taking photos, choose from dozens of different postcards and choose some of your favorite St. Croix attractions, beaches, or wildlife. Postcards are great for framing, or they make great keepsakes for loved ones when you write them a note and mail the postcard from St. Croix while you are still here.

Whatever your personal choice for keepsakes or gifts, Purple Papaya is the place for you to start your shopping. Not only are they 'St. Croix's finest gift shop', but they are also the largest. The friendly Purple Papaya staff will help you find just what you are looking for, and you'll get a great deal too!

Location : Christiansted

Phone : (340) 713-9412

Email : purplepapaya_stx@hotmail.com

St. Croix's #1 Souvenir Gift Shop! Nestled in the heart of St. Croix Historic Downtown Christiansted, and embedded in the Hearts and Minds of everyone who has entered through its doors, is The Purple Papaya Souvenir and Gift Shop. The store is loaded with everything from a full line of souvenirs, cold drinks, the largest selection of Printed & Embroidered t-shirts and sweatshirts, Hawaiian shirts Designer dresses, sun tan lotions, sunglasses, towels, Sandals, hats and caps, Underwater cameras, batteries, quality beach and swim wear for the entire family and MUCH, MUCH, MORE.

Shop in Unique Boutiques

There is a shift happening on a global level to support local businesses, and here on St. Croix the majority of businesses are locally owned and operated. The lack of chain stores found on St. Croix provides the island with some wonderfully diverse local boutiques offering unique products, as well as personalized customer service. Shop for stylish island fashions, books, teas and spices, home decor, and locally made skincare products...the options are endless and ever changing!

Whatever you may be shopping for here on St. Croix, it is important to shop locally. Not only will you get a more personalized shopping experience from St. Croix's boutique shop owners, but shopping locally stimulates the local economy and reduces the overall environmental impact. Local business owners often sell local products, which helps preserve St. Croix's unique community and creates more jobs locally. They also do what they do because they are passionate about their products and their customers.

Looking to add a little flair to your wardrobe? Indulge in the feel of the tropics with a new sundress or island-themed shirt. If you are looking for something a little classier, perhaps for a special event, you can find that too! Stylish linen pants for him, or a special occasion dress for her. Once you find that perfect outfit, don't forget to accessorize! Complete your ensemble with a great pair of sandals or heels, a coordinating handbag, and maybe even a stylish hat. You will find that the St. Croix shop owners and their employees are happy to help you to find just the right style and flattering fit for you. From personal experience I can tell you that boutique shopping for clothing here on the island is like having a personal shopper, so enjoy the experience as well as your purchases.

Hitting the beach? Shop for a swimsuits and cover-ups in the latest styles. You may also want to add a little protection from the sun with a rash guard, some polarized sunglasses, or a fun hat. Shop for the whole family, and don't forget the sunblock, beach towels, and maybe a beach bag as a souvenir from St. Croix. You can also find flip flops, or water socks if you are going to be hitting some of the rockier beaches. You can find everything you need to hit the beach in style in several boutiques and shops right along Queen Cross Street near the boardwalk in Christiansted.

While shopping for new wearable fashions can be fun, St. Croix also offers some beautiful and unique home decor and accessories inspired by island living. You will find one-of-a-kind furnishings for both indoors and outdoors, brought on to St. Croix from exotic destinations like Bali. You can also find locally painted art, carved bowls, glass display cases full of seashells, and other accessories that will allow you to bring the feeling of the island into your home. You can also shop for beautiful throw pillows, textiles, and table linens made from effervescent designs that make each piece a true work of art.

While you are shopping around, don't miss out on some of the unique items you can find that are produced right here on St. Croix. You will find amazing skincare products made with natural ingredients like coconut oil and aloe, and scented with locally grown herbs and botanicals. If you enjoy reading, pick up a book written by a local author. You can find books that discuss the history and culture of St. Croix, or more fun books that describe peoples personal experiences with island living. You can also find gifts and specialty items for your pets (or your pet-sitter), so they won't be left out!

Another wonderful thing about St. Croix is the sense of community the island shares. In many local boutiques sales from specific products, or a portion of all sales, go to support local St. Croix charities. You will also see a lot of emphasis as you shop in sourcing locally grown and sustainable products or ingredients, recycling, and minimizing our impact on the environment. With 'up-cycling' being such a popular pastime these days, you can find unusual ornaments, jewelry, bags, coasters, and more that were created using found or recycled items. You can also find bush tea, hot sauces, and spice blends that use locally sourced ingredients that allow you to take a taste of St. Croix home with you.

Remember to shop local and support the island you love. As the saying goes: 'You can't buy happiness, but you can buy local and that's kind of the same thing.

Shop the Christiansted Antiques & Collectibles Fair

Christiansted, St. Croix is a picturesque waterfront town who's beautiful historic buildings house custom jewelers, art galleries, tour operators, boutiques, restaurants, and other local businesses. Twice a year in Limpricht Park, right in the heart of downtown Christiansted, many of the local artists and artisans, vendors and shoppers gather for the Christiansted Antiques and Collectibles Fair.

This biannual fair is hosted by the Christiansted Community Alliance (CCA), a group of residents, business and property owners, schools, churches, professionals and individuals that recognize the uniqueness of Christiansted and are working together to revitalize the town. This family-friendly event is a great way to support Christiansted and to do some shopping all at the same time!

Once each Spring and once each Fall, Limpricht Park on Christiansted's King Street comes to life with vendors, music, local food and drinks, and activities for the kids. Shopping at the Antiques and Collectibles

Fair includes some great vintage finds, antiques, collectibles, one-of-a-kind furniture, textiles, local art, and fantastic locally carved wood furniture and sculptures for your home. For the fashion fabulous you will undoubtedly find locally made jewelry, clothing, and unique scarves or fabrics. For those who enjoy cooking (or just eating) you can find local herbs and spices, local honey, locally made mead or wine, coconut oil, and even fresh herbs and fruit trees for planting. There are treasures for everyone!

If you want to bring the kids along don't worry, there are childrens activities offered throughout the day. While you shop, the kids can enjoy story time under the shade trees, or participate in arts and crafts. Most importantly, don't miss out on some of the delicious specialties from the food vendors! You can sample many of the local favorites like roti, pates, kallaloo, smoothies, ginger beer, sorrel tea, tamarind drink, and more. You can also indulge in something sweet like homemade pastries, cakes, cookies, breads or ginger candy. There are some benches available in Limpricht Park, so you can enjoy your lunch or sweet treats in the shade of the beautiful trees.

The Christiansted Antiques and Collectibles Fair is a delightful day of community mingling, unique shopping, locally made food, and family fun. Please make sure to check our Calendar of Events for the date and time of the next fair so you can join in the fun and help support Christiansted!

Weddings

Plan your dream wedding on the picturesque island of St. Croix, US Virgin Islands. Pick the perfect location, invite your family and friends, and celebrate island style. Everything you need to plan your wedding: from marriage application requirements to activities for your guests, we've got you covered.

Weddings the Island Way

One of the most compelling reasons to plan a destination wedding on St. Croix is the stunning venues our island has to offer. In addition to the picturesque white sand beaches you would expect in the Caribbean, St. Croix is home to a variety of postcard-worthy settings for your special day. From historic properties to resorts, from the rainforest to the sea, somewhere on the island you will find the perfect location for your dream wedding.

If you want the quintessential Caribbean beach wedding, one of St. Croix's beautiful resort beaches is likely your best bet. The resorts keep their beaches clean, and also offer the facilities that you will want to have available to your guests, like parking and restrooms. Another added benefit to a resort beach wedding is that you can often get a package deal, as well as getting special room rates for your guests.

Historical places have an inexplicable romantic presence about them; perhaps because they have stood the test of time, a poignant symbol of your future lifetime together. Let the romantic aura of one of St. Croix's historic sites enhance the ambiance of your special day. Incorporate the culture and history of the island into your ceremony by getting married in an iconic sugarmill, one of two historic forts, or among the ruins of an 18th century plantation.

For the more traditional at heart, there are plenty of churches here on St. Croix where you can have a religious ceremony. St. Croix is known as the 'Land of Churches' since the island is home to approximately 150 churches, so if you dream of a church wedding you can choose one the island's many historic and beautiful churches.

St. Croix is also home to lush, subtropical rainforest and the unique flowers and foliage that come with that climate. If you like the feel of standing in the cool shade provided by towering trees, and the subtle fragrance of tropical flowers and dripping moss, the botanical gardens or a private villa may be your ideal venue. Or, enjoy the feel of a tropical garden in a secluded courtyard right in the heart of historic downtown Christiansted.

If you love the ocean, consider getting married out on the Caribbean Sea...or under it! You can celebrate your nuptials aboard one of Big Beard's catamarans for a sunset ceremony with your friends and family, or just the two of you. For the more adventurous, you can dive in say 'I do' underwater at one of St. Croix's stunning dive sites with Captain Ed (owner/operator of St. Croix Ultimate Bluewater Adventures) officiating.

The possibilities for your wedding ceremony and reception locations are endless, and they all make breathtaking backdrops for memories (and photos) that will last a lifetime. Make your St. Croix destination wedding everything you've ever dreamed it could be...and consider staying for the honeymoon!

My St. Croix Destination Wedding

Some of the best wedding planning inspiration comes from real life weddings. I have had the pleasure of planning my own destination wedding here on St. Croix. While I am a resident of St. Croix, most of our guests, 70 out of 80 to be exact, came from off island. It was a St. Croix destination wedding for everyone, except the bride and groom. I'd like to share a little about my St. Croix wedding with you, all the way from the proposal.

The Proposal
After a wonderful day of hiking and exploring, CJ took me for a romantic walk down the Frederiksted Pier at sunset. It was the very

same place where he had first set foot on St. Croix, one year prior, and fell in love with the island. During that sunset stroll, the man who had taken me on this crazy adventure to St. Croix got down on one knee and asked me to marry him.

The Planning

After eight months of living on St. Croix, CJ and I were engaged to be married. It didn't take long to decide that we wanted to have the wedding on St. Croix as well, so that we could share our fabulous island home with our friends and family. From the start, we knew we wanted a laid back, toes-in-the-sand kind of wedding. Not too serious, beach casual and fun. We wanted our friends and family to see why we love St. Croix. So we set out to plan a long wedding weekend to give our guests a taste of island life.

We opted to hire a wedding planner to help us through the process and I must say it was such a great help. Having a wedding planner to consult with and who already had connections with local vendors made researching and planning a whole lot easier. During the planning stages, our wedding planner was an invaluable resource not only for suggesting vendors but for keeping our planning focused and making sure we hadn't forgotten anything. When the week of the wedding arrived, all I had to do was make sure the wedding planner had all of our vendor information and contracts and it was her job to make sure everything happened on time and as planned. It was such a huge relief to know that everything was being taken care of, the decorations were being set, the deliveries were scheduled and on time and all I had to worry about was enjoying my day.

The Week of the Wedding

Guests began arriving on Monday the week of our wedding. Tuesday night, we invited close family, the wedding party, and a few island friends over for a cook-out. We threw some burgers and dogs on the grill and I put everyone to work. I had fifty welcome bags that needed to be assembled, so I let everyone help! Our welcome bags included a map, some island information and brochures, drink cozies, snacks, mini rum nips and mixers. By Wednesday, the majority of guests had arrived and they were eager to explore. We had an impromptu mid-day excursion with about 30 of our guests who were looking for something to do. We headed to La Reine Chicken Shack for their island specialty, rotisserie chicken and johnny cakes. After filling up, we moved on to the Cruzan Rum Distillery to take their factory tour. The inexpensive ($5) tour leads you through the actual rum making process as it's happening and finishes off with free samples! For having been thrown together at the last minute, it was one of the big hits of the week.

The Welcome Dinner

After the rehearsal, CJ's parents hosted a Welcome Dinner for all the guests at Cheeseburgers in America's Paradise. Guests were provided "Hi-My-Name-Is" name tags when they arrived and were encouraged to write how they knew the bride or groom along with their name. There were also trivia cards for guests to complete together, one with trivia about St. Croix and the other about Sam & CJ. The welcome dinner was the perfect opportunity to introduce everyone the wedding party and family members and for all of our guests to gather in a fun, casual setting and share a meal. The casual, family-style, picnic table atmosphere was perfect for mingling and getting acquainted, but it also gave CJ and I a chance to connect with everyone that had traveled to see us.

The Venue
Both the ceremony and reception were held at The Palms at Pelican Cove. CJ and I instantly loved everything about the resort the first time we visited. The location was ideal , situated on the North Shore, just minutes from Christiansted. Also ideal were the neighboring accommodations. While some guests stayed at The Palms, it's neighboring properties are the Hibiscus Beach Resort and a condo community that offers vacation rentals. This gave our guests a range of options for their accommodations. What we loved about The Palms was the layout. The beautiful palm tree grove for the ceremony was

only steps from the restaurant. The buffet dinner was held inside the main open-air dining room and dancing was outside under the stars. The staff at The Palms was easy to work with, responsive, eager to please and willing to accommodate our every request.

The Ceremony

As guests arrived on the beach for the ceremony, they were encouraged to kick off their shoes, dig their toes into the sand, and help themselves to some lemonade or ice water. The aisle was decorated with palm fronds and flowers. The ceremony began at 5 pm and the palm grove was wonderfully shady. Our officiant was Captain Steve from Big Beard's Adventure Tours (an ordained minister and friend of ours). He gladly let us customize our ceremony and write our own vows. One of CJ's brothers/groomsmen played acoustic guitar for our ceremony music. We chose yellow calla lilies for the bouquets and boutonnieres. My dad walked me down the aisle, cracking jokes the whole way. CJ and I exchanged vows and rings, I kissed my groom and we walked down the aisle together as Mr. & Mrs. to "Here Comes the Sun."

The Reception

A cocktail hour kicked off the festivities with libations and hors d'oeuvres. We chose to offer a limited bar serving rum punch, a red and a white wine and two types of beers; Sam Adams Lagar (where we came from) and Virgin Islands Ale (where we landed). The hors d'oeuvres served were coconut shrimp, bacon wrapped scallops, goat cheese & caramelized onion crustini, and fruit skewers with yogurt dip. After cocktail hour, we were seated for dinner. One of my bridesmaids, one of CJ's groomsmen, and my father gave beautiful and heartfelt toasts. Dinner was served buffet style offering tasty dishes with island flare. The dinner was topped off with the cutting of the cake, a simple white cake with mango filling decorated with palm trees and fresh flowers.

The Party

After dinner, we surprised our guests with a Mocko Jumbie performance. Even my parents didn't know about it! This was perfect for getting everyone out of their seats, onto the dance floor, and ready to party. The dance floor was strung with twinkle lights and paper lanterns to light the dance floor. The night flew by filled with dancing, laughter, congratulations, newly wed kisses and joy. It's still all a blur in my mind. CJ ended up in the pool thanks to his friends and brothers followed by the bridesmaids who just wanted to go for a dip.

The Boat Charter

The day after the wedding, we chartered one of Big Beard's boats, The Adventure, to take us and our guests to Buck Island for a 1/2 day trip. We took the afternoon trip to give ourselves and our guests a chance to sleep in after a late night of celebrating. Guests were encouraged to bring snacks and refreshments for the trip. Snorkel gear and instruction were provided by the crew. Captain Steve, the same one who'd married us the night before, was also our fearless boat captain. We stopped at the gorgeous Turtle Beach to put our toes in the soft white sand and then snorkeled the famous underwater snorkeling trail inside the reef. What a relaxing way to spend the day with our friends and family. We got to show everyone why we moved to St. Croix.

I couldn't have asked for a more perfect wedding week. It was exactly what we had wanted; laid-back, surrounded by the people we care about, sharing the beauty of St. Croix. Our friends and family are still talking about our St. Croix destination wedding.

Activity Ideas for Wedding Guests and Newlyweds

While you are not required to plan every day of your wedding guests trips, it is nice to have some group activities and optional excursions planned for while they are here. Many of your guests may be piggy-backing their family vacation onto your big day, so leave some time for guests to do their own thing too. But remember, they have come all this way to celebrate with you and you should offer some activity options for them.

Group activities provide a great opportunity for guests to mingle and get to know each other too! We've put together a few suggestions for fun and engaging group activities so your guests can experience St. Croix.

Welcome Dinner

A great idea to get all of your guests acquainted is to host a Welcome Dinner in lieu of a Rehearsal Dinner. Traditionally, out of town guests are invited to the rehearsal dinner along with the wedding party and immediate family. Having a destination wedding means all of your guests are from out of town, so it's best to include everyone. By having a Welcome Dinner you can gather all of your guests together before the big event so that you can connect with each of them and they can get acquainted with one another. This can range from a fancy seated dinner to a super casual gathering at a burger joint or beach bar. (Don't forget to discuss who is hosting this event while you're budgeting.)

Central Meeting Place

Designating a central meeting place can help your guests find one another each day while they are here. This could be the breakfast buffet at the hotel you're staying at or a casual daily activity like a morning trip to the beach or walk around the hotel property.

Shopping Parties

Plan a trip to Christiansted with your wedding party or a group of friends for a fun day of strolling the streets and exploring the shops.

Pick up those last minute attendant gifts, shop for some new island wear, or pick up a souvenir to take home, set up an exclusive Private Shopping Party for you and your friends. Make a day of it! Plan to grab lunch at a downtown restaurant and have the rest of your group meet you for afternoon cocktails.!

A Trip to Buck Island

A must-see while on St. Croix, day trips to Buck Island are popular among wedding parties. They offer a fun day on the water, a chance to spend quality time with your guests, and a glimpse into the underwater world around St. Croix. There are several great companies that can take you to Buck Island, and each one can customize the experience for your group. Half day or full day, sailing or motor boat, and more. Any of the Captains will be happy to work with you to provide a fabulous trip for you and your guests. For more info about licensed companies ready to take your group to Buck Island, .

Caribbean Night

Sit back and let someone else do the planning. Several resorts on St. Croix host themed Caribbean Nights weekly. This is a fun and easy way to get your group together for a dinner buffet and entertainment that may include a variety of cultural performances like Mocko Jumbies, Fire Dancing, and more.

Island Tours

While you and your guests are on St. Croix, you might as well take a look around! An island tour is a great way to get to know this wonderful place where you've chosen to get married. And there are many styles of guided tours available to best suit your group's level of fitness, adventure, and interests. An open-air safari bus, dirt road ATV tours, bicycle tours, farm tours, walking tours through St. Croix's historic towns, kayak tours by day or night. You can even hire a local guide to take your group on a hike that includes ecology and botany. An island tour will give your guests some history and insight into St. Croix..

Golfing

This is a great activity to get guests together for an outing. People form great bonds over a round of golf. Think about mixing and matching some foursomes so that your guests can get to know each other better. There are 2 world-class golf courses, as well as a 9 hole course. There's even mini-golf if your group skews younger with children.

Brunch

After a long weekend of celebrations, sleep in Sunday morning and then meet everyone for Sunday Brunch. Brunch is big on St. Croix and plenty of restaurants offer great options. If you've got a big group interested in going, make sure to call ahead for reservations! Our picks for brunch: Angry Nate's, Beach Side Cafe, and The Palms.

Relax
After all the planning, traveling, and spending time with your guests, it's time to treat yourselves to some pampering. You and your spouse can run off together for a couples massage. Whether on the beach, your hotel room or private villa it will surely be the escape you are looking for. .

Don't forget to check out our list of 100 Things To Do on St. Croix for even more ideas! Enjoy your time on St. Croix!

Underwater Wedding

St. Croix residents John Santino and Toni Wilson made history in 2010...by breaking the Guinness Book of World Records for the largest underwater wedding. 103 certified divers, including the bride and groom, submerged for the brief nuptials at Rainbow Beach, easily surpassing the existing record of 39 underwater guests.

To verify their presence, guests signed slates both above and below the ocean's surface. The large number of sand-stirring witnesses and the season's weather conditions limited visibility, yet the "I Dos" were all spelled out on laminated sheets of paper that the couple used for their vows.

After officiant, Captain John Macy, signaled to the newlyweds that they were now married, Toni, John, and all their companions surfaced to greet dry guests at the Rainbow Beach Bar, where rum and cokes and hamburgers completed the affair. Talk about an island-style wedding! Toni had her dream wedding, and it was stress free.

When asked why the couple decided on an underwater wedding, the bride said: "I didn't want to plan a 'real' wedding." This was indeed a real wedding, a great news story, and a wonderful way for St. Croix to go down in history as the location for the world's largest Underwater Wedding.If you are thinking about an underwater wedding, consider St. Croix! With beautiful beaches, great Caribbean diving, and several qualified officiants, St. Croix offers everything you need to say "I do" below the big ol' blue.

Location : Island Wide

Phone : (340) 773-4482

Website : www.bigbeards.com/weddings/

The Perfect Venue for a Wedding In Paradise! Think of the Big Beard's yacht as your own private chapel, with scenic backdrops like the sun setting over the Caribbean, Buck Island's secluded beach, the lush hills of St. Croix, and historic Christiansted harbor. Big Beard's Weddings in Paradise will accommodate your wishes and create the perfect

Caribbean wedding on shore, or on the high seas. Choose from several packages with one of their licensed ministers, or create your own dream wedding. You can also charter their yacht for a post-rehearsal sunset sail, as a fun excursion for your destination wedding guests

Beaches

We've tackled the hard task of visiting each and every St. Croix beach to let you know the best beaches to swim, snorkel, take a walk, bring the kids, or just relax with your toes in the sand. The wonderful thing about St. Croix beaches is that they are all public. You are allowed access to all beaches, but be mindful of restrictions or fees. Certain beaches are protected and access restricted because of turtle habitats and nesting, while you may need to pay an amenities fee to use a hotel or resort beach. Browse through our beach directory below to find the St. Croix beaches that best suit your beach desire. Visit one, or explore them all!

Gentle Winds

Gentle Winds Beach is located on the North Shore of St. Croix, between Salt River and Cane Bay. This beach is home to the private Gentle Winds condominium community. While the beach itself is public (by law), access to the beach through Gentle Winds is limited to residents and guests of the community. The beach is also accessible by boat, but please be cautious as there is a shallow reef just off the beach. All amenities located on the beach are also for the use of residents and guests only.

Amenities
There is parking, restrooms, a beachside fresh water pool, beach and snack bar, beach chairs, umbrellas, and hammocks available, but they are for residents and guests only.

Directions
Located on the North Shore between Salt River and Cane Bay at the Gentle Winds condominium community.

Restrictions
All amenities, including parking on the premises, are restricted to use by the residents and guests of the Gentle Winds condominiums only.

Dorsch

This beautiful stretch of sandy beach is just south of Frederiksted, past the fish market. Dorsch Beach features soft, white sand and plenty of shade under palm and sea grape trees, making it a great place to relax and spend the day. Dorsch Beach is a favorite with locals on the weekends and holidays, but is generally nice and quiet during the weekdays. With a mostly sandy bottom, there is not much to see while snorkeling except around the small rocky patches. However, the calm waters of the West End are great for swimming and floating. Also, offshore there are several dive sites that can be reached by boat or by shore. With a great view of Frederiksted Pier, Dorsch Beach is also a fantastic location to watch the sunset.

Amenities

Dorsch Beach itself does not offer any amenities, but it is a short walk to the town of Frederiksted where you can find multiple restaurants, bars, shops, dive shops, and more. Dorsch Beach also runs along Sand Castle on the Beach resort, where you can purchase a day pass for the use of their beachside chairs, umbrellas, restrooms, bar, and freshwater pool.

Directions

Drive south from Frederiksted on Veterans Shore Drive, staying along the water. Once you pass the fish market and boat launch, you can park anywhere along the road.

Restrictions

None.

Frederiksted

Frederiksted Beach, also known as Fort Frederik Beach, is located in the town of Frederiksted just north of the Pier and Fort Frederik (across the street from the ballpark). It is the most easily accessible beach from the cruise ship pier. An easy stroll around the front of the fort puts you on Frederiksted Beach. There are some trees here that provide relief from the sun, and the park across the street is a great spot for young kids to play. With public restrooms, picnic tables, and plenty of space to spread out, you could easily spend the entire day here, relax, and then watch sunset. Keep in mind that this beach can be crowded when there is a ship in port.

The northern end of this beach offers every amenity you could ask for a restaurant and bay, a board shop with rentals and lessons, chair and umbrella rentals. You may also want to try your hand at fishing at this beach. Frederiksted Beach can be rocky in places, but there are places to enter to swim just watch out below for sea urchins! This beach has calm water, making this a area for paddle boarding, swimming and snorkeling. Make sure to keep a look out in the clear, shallow water for octopus, flounder, butterfly fish, angel fish and blue tangs.

Amenities
Lots of parking along the beach and across the street next to the ballpark. There is a restaurant and bar, public restrooms, chair and umbrella rentals, a board shop offering surf, skim, skate, stand up paddle board rentals and lessons, and snorkel gear rentals available.

Directions

If walking from the cruise ship pier, follow the path around the front of Fort Frederik to get to the beach. If driving, drive north through town past Fort Frederik. There is parking along the street across from the ballpark.

Monk's Bath Tidal Pools & Northside Valley Beach

Northside Valley Beach and the Monk's Bath Tidal Pools are located on the northwest corner of St. Croix, near Northside Valley. This beach is very secluded and more than likely you'll have the whole place to yourself. Northside Valley Beach is tiny and mostly rocky, but great for exploring and snorkeling. Hike towards the north and you will find the Monk's Bath Tidal Pools. We recommend wearing shoes, as the rock formations can be very sharp. If you are up for an adventure, the rocky shoreline makes for incredible snorkeling. Just be careful when entering and exiting the water as urchins like to live in the crevices. Since the terrain is precarious, we recommend you take someone with you for safety reasons if you choose to go here.

Amenities

There are no amenities here. Bring plenty of drinking water and sun protection, and wear sturdy shoes since the rock and coral formations can be very sharp.

Directions

This beach is located 3 miles north of the town of Frederiksted. Once you pass the Northside Valley sign, drive about 1/4 mile further until you see a large facility building on the right. Park on the left side of the road, but don't leave valuables in the car.

Rainbow

Rainbow Beach is located on the west end of St. Croix. There is plenty of parking available and a restaurant/bar where you can order food and drinks. There is usually live music, and a volleyball net set up on the beach for players. This is the Sunday hang out spot on St. Croix, otherwise referred to as 'Sunday Funday'. If you're looking for peace and quiet, you may want to try another beach. This beach is a popular destination on cruise ship days as well.

The water does have a rocky bottom in places, so watch where you step. The water is typically calm, so this is a good spot for snorkeling, and paddle boarding, and there are jet ski rentals located here. There isn't much shade, unless you go up to the restaurant area, so be sure to pack some sunblock and an umbrella if you're going to want relief from the sun.

Amenities

Lots of parking is available along the beach and across the street. There is a restaurant and bar with restrooms available to patrons, and a water sports shop offering jet-ski rentals and tours, as well as stand up paddle board, kayak, float, and snorkel gear rentals, and beach chair and umbrella rentals.

Sand Castle

Sand Castle Beach is located a half mile south of the Frederiksted Pier and is home to two hotels, Sand Castle on the Beach and Cottages by the Sea. It is a gorgeous long stretch of beach with some structure for snorkeling. Sand Castle Beach has serenely calm waters, perfect for swimming, kayaking, paddle boarding or snorkeling. Plan to spend the day here, rent some beach chairs and an umbrella for shade and treat yourself to lunch at the beach side restaurant and bar.

For cruise ship passengers, it's an easy walk from the cruise ship pier. A day pass is available for cruise ship passengers or those who wish to camp out and enjoy a beach day. You can purchase a day pass from Sand Castle on the Beach for $25, which includes 2 chairs and an umbrella, towels, 2 refreshing glasses of rum punch, and access to the hotel amenities including the beach side freshwater pool, outdoor shower, and restrooms.

Amenities

At Sand Castle on the Beach you will find a bar and restaurant, chair and umbrella rentals, restrooms, and a freshwater pool available, but for hotel guests and day pass holders only. As with all beaches on St. Croix, this is a public beach, but if you choose to access the beach without the amenities available through the hotel make sure to bring your own sun protection, water and a beach chair or mat.

Directions

From Frederiksted, drive south along the water. You will see signs for Sand Castle on the Beach about 1/2 mile south of the Frederiksted Pier. Convenient parking is available at the hotel, or parking is available in the lot across the street.

Restrictions

Chairs, umbrellas, pool access, restrooms, and other hotel amenities are for hotel guests and day pass holders only. The beach is freely accessible, but in order to take advantage of these services you must purchase a beach pass.

Sandy Point

The official name of the beach is Sandy Point National Wildlife Refuge. Sandy Point is located on the West End of St. Croix. Simply put, this beach is absolutely stunning. It boasts crystal clear blue water and a 2 mile long stretch of sandy white beach (one of the longest in the Caribbean). This beach is typically not crowded, it's likely that you'll be one of the only ones there. There is little to no shade here however, and there are no facilities here. This beach is only open on the weekends (including holiday weekends) and when there is a cruise ship in port, with the exception of April-August when it is closed entirely due to turtle nesting season. All this exclusivity, however, makes Sandy Point even more rewarding when it is open.

We don't recommend going to this remote beach alone. You cannot put stake anything into the ground, namely an umbrella, so your only protection from the sun is good ol' sunscreen which is highly recommended. The water has a drop off and gets very deep very quick. There is no fringe reef off of Sandy Point and the sea has a deep sandy bottom, so if you are snorkeling you won't see as much here as other places, but keep your eyes peeled for turtles and rays in these waters. Just float your way to bliss at Sandy Point.

Turtle Watch

Sandy Point is a critical nesting habitat for the endangered leatherback sea turtle. Between the months of April-August, the beach is closed entirely to the public, and under strict watch by Rangers of the U.S. Fish and Wildlife Department. During the months of active turtle nesting, marine biologists and rangers manage an intensive research program. Volunteers tag and collect data on nesting turtles and help to relocate turtle nests away from erosion zones when necessary. Sandy Point provides habitat for over 100 species of birds as well. Bring your binoculars to spot brown pelicans, black-necked stilts, and yellow warblers, among others.

Sandy Point in Film, Commercials, and Videos
You may not realize that you've seen this beach before — in the movie Shawshank Redemption, starring Tim Robbins and Morgan Freeman. It was the runaway film success of 1994, based on a short story by Stephen King. Most of the movie takes place in a prison, except the memorable scenes that in the film that supposedly take place in Zihuatanejo (Mexico), but really are St. Croix, USVI. The last scene of the movie was filmed at Sandy Point, as have been numerous television commercials and photo shoots for catalogs.

Amenities
There are no amenities at Sandy Point. Make sure to bring plenty of drinking water, sun protection, and food if necessary. There is very little shade, so plan accordingly.

Directions & Parking
From mid-island, take Melvin Evans Highway west. Continue straight, the highway will turn into a two way road. Along this road, you will see

the entrance gate into Sandy Point National Wildlife Refuge. Enter through the gate and follow the dirt road past the salt ponds. There are several parking areas within the refuge with access to the beach.

Restrictions
Because Sandy Point is a critical nesting habitat for the endangered leatherback sea turtle, access to the beach is restricted to Saturday and Sunday from 10 am 4 pm only, and is closed to the public from April 1st through August 31st for nesting season. Pets are not allowed, and nothing can be staked/anchored into the sand including umbrellas, chairs, or pop-ups

Cane Bay

Cane Bay Beach is a popular hang out for locals and visitors alike. It is also a popular place for families to hang out with their kids, and dogs, because it's a one stop beach that has everything. With access to several bars and restaurants right from the beach, it makes for an easy and enjoyable beach day. There is plenty to do to keep you occupied. Bask in the Caribbean sun, play volleyball, rent some beach chairs and dive into a good book, or take a dip in the clear warm water. Scuba diving and snorkeling are a popular pastimes here, as Cane Bay offers easy access from the shore.

This beach can get busy on the weekends with restaurants offering specials and live entertainment, and many families barbecuing or having birthday parties on the beach. We highly enjoying a meal or a cold cocktail at Eat @ Cane Bay. Cane Bay is also where the annual Mardi Croix parade and celebration takes place, a St. Croix tradition very similar to Mardi Gras.

Scuba Diving

Cane Bay is rated one of the top dive locations in the Caribbean, and deservedly so. There is a dive shop on premises that has been in business more than twenty years. They offer scuba instruction, guided shore dives, boat dives, night dives, as well as scuba gear rental and snorkel gear rentals. If you're not already a certified diver, you'd be fortunate to discover it here, or get certified at this very special location. Dive the famous "Wall", where the ocean floor turns into a steep cliff that drops more than 2 miles deep along the Puerto Rico Trench. The shelf and the wall are perfect for seeing many species of fish, turtles, moray eels, garden eels, shrimp, squid, lobster, crabs, seahorses, reef sharks, maybe even the occasional dolphin or humpback whale if you're lucky, and so much more! This is also home to a grant-funded coral restoration project. Not ready to try diving? Rent some snorkel gear and swim out to the living coral garden with both hard and soft corals.

Amenities

Within walking distance of Cane Bay Beach are three restaurants and bars, two of them right on the beach, offering lunch, dinner and drinks. Chair rentals are available right on the beach. In addition to the dive shop where you can rent dive or snorkel gear, there are kayak tours and rentals nearby, as well as horseback riding tours.

Parking is available in the small parking lot across the street, but street parking is acceptable too. Restrooms are available to patrons of the restaurants.

Directions

Cane Bay Beach is located on the North Shore of St. Croix, about 5 miles west of Salt River Bay

Columbus Landing

Columbus Landing Beach is located on the North Shore of the island, within the Salt River Bay Historical and Ecological Preserve. This beach was the site of a native village in the 1400's and is historically significant because of the encounter between Christopher Columbus' crew with the natives in his second journey to the America's in 1493. There is a visitors center on the hill, accessible by dirt road (beware of large ruts and potholes). There is a short, easy trail through some tall grass that leads to the site of an earthen fort. This lookout affords beautiful views of Salt River Bay. There are several kayak companies in the area that offer tours of Salt River Bay and extensive historical insight into the area. Because this is a National Historical Landmark, please do not take any souvenirs or leave any trash behind.

This is a fairly secluded beach and doesn't see very much traffic. More times than not, you will be the only ones there. The water is good for swimming and there is reef just a short way out for snorkeling. Otherwise, there is generally a grassy bottom with sporadic sandy parts. There is also some great diving located offshore, and several local dive shops offer boat dives in this area. There are no amenities here and there is little shade, so be sure to pack your sun protection.

Amenities
There are no amenities on the Columbus Landing Beach aside from a few thatch awnings for shade. There is a visitors center on the hill with restrooms a short drive away. Be sure to bring lots of drinking water and sun protection.

Directions
From Christiansted, take Northside Road through La Grande Princesse and turn right onto North Shore Road. The entrance for Salt River Marina will be on your right hand side. Take the road past Salt River Marina. This road will dead end at Columbus Landing.

Restrictions

Access to Salt River Bay Historical and Ecological Preserve and the Columbus Landing site is restricted to day use only. Digging, littering and the construction of temporary structures is prohibited and punishable by fines. The Salt River Bay Historical and Ecological Preserve is co-managed by the Virgin Islands Department of Planning and Natural Resources, the National Park Service and the Government of the Virgin Islands.

Pelican Cove

Pelican Cove Beach, also known as Cormorant Beach, is located on the North Shore of St. Croix, only a short drive from Christiansted. Home to two hotels and a condominium complex, Pelican Cove's long stretch of sandy beach dotted with swaying palm trees has something to offer for everyone. With two restaurants serving breakfast, lunch, dinner and drinks daily, restrooms, beach chairs, free parking, natural shade from trees, beach volleyball, kayaks for hotel guests, great snorkeling and more, Pelican Cove is the perfect place to spend a day or a whole week.

Parts of Pelican Cove Beach may be rocky, but there are areas conducive to swimming, just be aware as there can be strong current in this area. There is a stretch of reef just off the beach that is great for snorkeling. The towering palms lining the beach provide great natural shade, should you want to escape from the sun. The area of Pelican Cove Beach inside The Palms at Pelican Cove Resort in Little Princess, has been awarded the internationally recognized Blue Flag Award.

Amenities
There are two restaurants on the beach serving breakfast, lunch, dinner, and drinks. There are beach chairs available for hotel guests. Snorkeling equipment and kayaks may be available for hotel guests be sure to ask the hotel about use. There are bathrooms available at both hotel restaurants for patrons. Parking is free at both establishments as well.

Directions
From Christiansted, head West out of town on King Street. Turn right at the light onto Northside Road / Route 75 past Pueblo supermarket. At the next light (Five Corners) make a slight left turn to stay on Northside Road. After about 1 mile, turn right at Gas City (look for the red gas station sign). You can either follow signs for Hibiscus Beach Resort or The Palms at Pelican Cove. Each has beach access and parking.

Restriction

Beach chairs, snorkel equipment, kayaks and other amenities may be reserved for hotel guests and restaurant patrons. Be sure to check with staff members before use.

Annaly Bay and Tide Pools

ALERT: Please consider going with a trained guide as the terrain can be quite precarious. Also, be sure to check the wind and sea conditions before taking this adventure.

Annaly Bay Beach and Tide Pools are located on the North Shore, over the hill from Carambola Resort. Access to these enchanting tide pools is somewhat difficult. You either have to hike here, or take a vehicle that has 4-wheel drive down to the beach and hike from there. However, the road is difficult to navigate so make sure you know what you're doing, or hire an off roading tour company that does, if you choose to drive there. The hike is somewhat difficult, so make sure to keep that in mind. We promise, once you get here all your effort will be worth it. Breathtaking is an understatement. You will be fully surrounded by nature and all its beauty at these gorgeous tidal pools.

If you choose to make the hike, park your car at Carambola Resort and there are signs marking where the hiking trail begins, and if you're unsure check with the guard at the guard-gate. The 5 mile round trip hike is through the rain forest, so it is mostly in shade, but the trail is steep at parts. We recommend wearing sturdy shoes and bringing plenty of drinking water and maybe a snack. There are no facilities so you are on your own. Keeping that in mind, and the fact that this location is so remote, take extra care to ensure you and others don't hurt yourselves (it's a long way back to civilization). Also, there is not much shade here, so make sure you pack lots of water and sunscreen for this venture. The beach at the end of the hike is comprised of smooth rocks and pebbles instead of sand not great for swimming and the surf can be quite rough. The real draw of taking the time to get to Annaly Bay are the tidal pools. At the far west end of the beach you will need to climb over the rocks to get to the tidal pools. The tidal pools are a beautiful spot to rest and take a dip to cool off. There are more pools than just the first large one you can continue climbing to the west to find more. Use your best judgement: if the waves are too rough, don't risk the climb.

Amenities
Before starting the hike into Annaly Bay Beach and the Tide Pools, you can access parking, restrooms, and the bars/restaurants at the Renaissance Carambola Beach Resort. However, there are NO amenities down at Annaly Bay, so bring plenty of drinking water, food and sun protection. Please keep in mind that this is a very remote location, so take every precaution when hiking and swimming.

Directions

To find the trail head, drive along the north shore all the way west until you find Renaissance Carambola Beach Resort. Park your car in the upper lot, outside of the guard gate. The trail head is at the edge of the bush, marked Trumble Trail with a sign. Ask at the guard gate if you're not sure. The trail is fairly well maintained and easy to follow. When you reach the beach, follow the beach to the left and over the rocks to reach the tidal pools. If you're not up for the hike, there are jeep tours that will take you there. We don't recommend trying to drive there yourself

Davis Bay

Davis Bay Beach, otherwise known as Carambola Beach, is located on the North Shore. This picturesque beach is home to Renaissance Carambola Beach Resort. With an ample stretch of white sand surrounded by verdant hills, Davis Bay is truly paradise. Here there are rolling hills, lots of palm trees, and rocky cliffs being sprayed by the ocean mist of crashing waves. Head on down to the beach for a relaxing day of limin' in the sun with a good book, or enjoy the water activities available onsite. If this sounds wonderful, then you've found your beach.

It is a resort beach, so there are beach chairs and hammocks tucked among the trees for guest use. Even better, utilize the onsite dive shop and snorkel equipment rentals or have lunch at the beach side bar and restaurant. Okay, if that didn't get you...golf and tennis courts are also onsite for guests. That being said, please be aware that the beach has a rocky bottom in some areas and often strong currents, so please be careful if you choose to swim here. Swimming and snorkeling are great when the conditions are right, but the surf can get rough and the currents can be strong.

Amenities
The resort offers parking, a restaurant and bar, restrooms, a dive shop, snorkel rentals, chairs and hammocks.

Directions
Drive along the north shore all the way west until you see signs for Renaissance Carambola Beach Resort. If you are not a guest of the resort, park your car in the upper parking lot outside the guard gate. There public beach access just outside the resort ask at the guard at the gate if you need help locating it. Follow the signs at the bottom of the steps to get to the beach. Or, drive past the guard gate and park in their hotel/beach parking lot.

Restrictions
The beach chairs and hammocks are reserved for guests only.

Shoys

Shoys Beach is on the East End of St. Croix, conveniently located just a few miles outside of Christiansted. Quiet and secluded, Shoys Beach is a picturesque stretch of white sand overlooking the Caribbean waters and makes for a great getaway. Parts of the beach are a little rocky, but there are plenty of sandy areas as well. The waters are calm for most of the year and the bottom is generally sandy and grassy which makes for great swimming conditions. Shoys Beach is frequented by locals, part-time residents, regular visitors, and vacationers alike. There are no amenities at this beach, there is however plenty of shade from the seagrape trees and other foliage that lines the beach.

If you bring your snorkeling gear with you, there is some decent snorkeling, particularly along the easternmost part of the bay where there is a small reef (just look for the area where the waves are breaking). In the rocky areas, look for lobster, small eels and tropical fish, and in the sandy, grassy areas look for rays, conch and the occasional trumpet fish. The water is usually pretty calm, however a few waves can develop occasionally if one wishes to body surf. Shoys Beach is also a nice, long stretch of beach for walking or running.

Amenities

Parking is available, but there are no amenities at Shoys Beach. Bring plenty of drinking water, sun protection, food, and your beach chair or mat.

Directions

Head east out of Christiansted along East End Road. Turn left at the entry into The Buccaneer Hotel property. There will be two guard gates: the one straight ahead will take you to the hotel; the gate to the right is the entrance to Estate Shoys. Approach the gate to the right and let the guard know you are headed to the beach (they will ask for your name and then allow you access to this gated neighborhood). Follow the main road around until it dead ends, there you will find a gravel parking area on the right side of the road park your vehicle here. Directly across from the parking area is the beach access path, marked by a small sign. Follow this short path through the bush to reach the Shoys Beach.

Restrictions

None. However, please be respectful of the surrounding private properties as Estate Shoys is a residential neighborhood.

Turtle Beach, Buck Island

Turtle Beach is on the West Side of Buck Island, located about one and a half miles off the northeast coast of St. Croix...and it is beyond gorgeous. It is a long stretch of sugary white sand and crystal clear waters. Lay on the sun-kissed sand and bask in the warmth of the suns rays. The current here is generally calm, and makes for a great spot to swim and test out your snorkel gear. You can also choose to go for a stroll along the beach, or if you're feeling up to it hiking up the island. If you choose to partake in the hike, please make sure you pack good walking shoes. There is not much shade provided on this island oasis, so be sure to pack your sunscreen and a hat.

Buck Island is protected by the National Park and is uninhabited by people. Sail through the turquoise waters of the lagoon over to the East Side of the island for the wonderful snorkeling; here is where you will find the famous underwater trail. You will see schools of Blue Tang, Parrotfish, Angelfish, and many other beautiful and exotic fish as well. You may even spot a couple turtles. After the snorkeling, hop back on the boat for a relaxing sail back to the mainland of St. Croix. For more information on Buck Island, please see our Buck Island page.

Amenities
There are restrooms, grills and a picnic area provided and maintained by the National Park Service.

Directions
Located on the West Side of Buck Island, accessible only by boat. There is no fee to access the island on a private boat, but a permit is

required. Tour operators also offer trips to Buck Island, however fees do vary for full or half day snorkeling excursions depending on the tour operator.

Restrictions

There is no overnight camping on the island and the park is closed from sunset to sunrise to protect nesting sea turtles that come ashore at night. Anchorage is available overnight to boaters within a designated area, but a permit is required to anchor within the designated area. Pets, vehicles (except wheelchairs) artificial light, camping, glass containers, generators, and loud music are prohibited. Build fires only in the grills provided by the National Park Service. Camping, digging tent poles, beach umbrellas, and stakes are prohibited on beaches.

Butler Bay

Butler Bay Beach is located on the West End of the island, just down the road from Sprat Hall. There are some tide pools that are the home to many small fish, and there is some good snorkeling to be found. It's remote location makes this beach a quiet and peaceful spot with plenty of sand to play in or to sunbathe on, and the water is generally calm due to it's West End location. Butler Bay also offers some shade trees for those wishing to stay cool. This beach has lots of rocks and tiny shells to peruse, and it is a nice beach to let your dog run around, but not necessarily great for open water swimming due to the sometimes strong currents. We do recommend going during the day as opposed to during the evening, and take someone with you due to the remote location.

If you are a diver, offshore at Butler Bay you will find five different wrecks to dive on. While you can reach some of the wrecks as a shore dive, they are easiest to reach by boat with one of the local dive shops, especially when the currents are strong.

Amenities
There are no amenities here. Bring plenty of drinking water and sun protection, and wear sturdy shoes if you are going to check out the tide pools since the rock and coral formations can be very sharp.

Directions
This beach is located north of the town of Frederiksted on Route 63 north of Creque Dam Road (Route 58) and Sprat Hall. You can park on the side of the road, but don't leave valuables in the car.

Family Fun

If you are looking for a fun, tropical family vacation, St. Croix is the place for you! Take the family for a day trip out to Buck Island where you can snorkel, float and enjoy a beach barbecue. Try a new water sport such as stand up paddle-boarding or kayaking. Want to take a break from the water? How about taking everyone on an ATV or a Tan Tan off-road tour of the rainforest? If you want something entertaining for the evening, take the kids out to one of the many restaurants or resorts that host hermit crab races…you can even bet on a crab to win prizes! And make sure your family catches one of St. Croix's many Caribbean nights where you can enjoy a dinner of local fare and see the iconic mocko jumbies. The possibilities for family fun are endless, the tough part is deciding which activity to do first!

5 Ways to Beat the Heat on St. Croix

During the summertime, it can be hot and muggy here on St. Croix. On the plus side, we are surrounded by the Caribbean Sea, so you can always take a dip to cool off. But, aside from heading to the beach, the island offers many other ways to keep your cool that don't involve getting sand everywhere. Whether you want something inside in air conditioned comfort, or you just need something to make the heat more tolerable, the island offers fun activities for adults and children of all ages that will help you keep your cool.

Here are five ways we here at GoToStCroix.com recommend beating the heat on this island of eternal summer:

1. **Lounge by a resort pool.**

If you would rather enjoy the fresh water of a pool, without sacrificing the Caribbean view, you can purchase a pool pass from one of several resorts here on St. Croix. Out west, Sand Castle on the Beach offers a pool pass for just $10 per person, which includes a fresh towel, beach chair and umbrella, access to the two pools, shower, changing room and bar/restaurant. As an added bonus, if you eat lunch at Beach Side Cafe restaurant, day passes are reduced to $5 per person! Or, you can head to The Palms at Pelican Cove on the North Shore who also offers a pool pass for just $10 a day ($5 a day for kids), which includes a credit towards food purchases at their restaurant. In either case, you can still enjoy a view of the Caribbean while lounging poolside.

2. Indulge in some ice cream or a smoothie.

There are several local places here on St. Croix that offer delicious, homemade ice cream and smoothies. Choose your favorite traditional flavor, or from tropical ice cream flavors made using locally sourced ingredients. Several local ice cream stops, like Jaccar Ice Cream & Desserts, also offer vegan options or low-sugar sorbets for those with dietary restrictions. If you want a healthier option than ice cream, smoothies made with local produce are a great way to go. Baked Cafe is currently offering "Smoothie Happy Hour" daily from 1pm-3pm, so you can get a fresh, local smoothie at a discounted price. Or, check out the Bar @ 340 in Golden Rock, the Seahorse Republic food truck or Seaside Market & Deli in Gallows Bay, or The Courtyard Juices & Fitness Studio in Christiansted to get your smoothie fix. To learn more,.

3. Jump off the Frederiksted Pier.

Plunging into the cool water surrounding the pier is refreshing and fun for all ages, but with none of the sand! There is an area midway down the Frederiksted Pier where you can jump off and then climb back up a partially submerged ladder. If you enjoy marine life, wear a pair of goggles or a mask and make sure to look around under the pier before you climb back up because there are a ton of sea creatures that make their homes on and around the pier pilings. Make sure to give yourself lots of time, because you will definitely want to jump more than once! Plus, you can cross #31 off your 100 Things To Do on St. Croix list!

4. Get a manicure or pedicure.

If you want to sit back and relax in air conditioned comfort, why not pamper yourself? Get a pedicure and beautify your feet so they look great in those flipflops, or get a manicure so your hands are even more eye-catching as you sip that tropical cocktail. Better yet, go for a mani/pedi combo! At Ruba's Nail Oasis you can relax and enjoy peace of mind knowing that they use only organic, natural products on your skin and nails, and all of the nail varnishes are non-toxic, vegan, eco-friendly and cruelty free. Or, enjoy the rejuvenating resort day spa experience while you pamper your hands and feet at Tamarind Reef Spa or The Buccaneer Hideway Spa.

5. Go rave bowling.

Bowling is a great way for the whole family to have fun together in air conditioned comfort...rave bowling is even more fun! Bowl in the glow of the neon lights while you enjoy a light show and a live DJ spins tunes on Saturday nights from 8:30pm-close at Tropical Ten Pins Bowling Center. There is even a restaurant and bar onsite, so you can really make a night of it.

These are just five of the many ways we locals beat the heat here on St. Croix, but there are many to choose from. However you choose to stay cool, enjoy the beautiful island setting and the wonderfully friendly people that make St. Croix the place to be, even when it's hot outside

Where to Get Your Ice Cream Fix

Whether you are looking for a plain scoop of ice cream, a scratch-made ice cream sandwich, a frozen treat low in sugar, or even vegan ice cream, St. Croix has it all! Even better, enjoy delicious tropical and seasonal flavors you won't find anywhere else. Don't worry, you can still get vanilla and chocolate ice cream with sprinkles, but you could also choose soursop, mango, coconut, or gooseberry. Here's the scoop on some of our favorite stops for ice cream...

Jaccar Ice Cream & Desserts

Get your ice cream fix at this charming little shop where the Hibbert family lovingly makes all of their ice cream on-site, using predominately locally-sourced ingredients. Jaccar offers ice cream by the scoop or container (ask about their Sustainable Scoops program), sundaes, low-sugar sorbet, vegan ice cream, popsicles, scratch-made ice cream sandwiches, and ice cream cakes. They have an ice cream cart to cater events, so consider them make ice cream for your next party!

Love-Croix Helados & Eatz

What started as a popular ice cream cart at local events has grown into a full on food truck, offering all kinds of delicious eats. But, just because they've expanded doesn't mean the helados (ice cream) has suffered. Stop by the lovely little shaded area Love-Croix owners Bulley and Marilyn Navarro have created in Peter's Rest for delicious, homemade helados in local flavors like mango and coconut. Great vibes and great ice cream!

Baked Cafe

With a passion for offering scratch made vegan and gluten-free foods made with fresh, local ingredients, Baked Cafe owner Alex Morris offers a flavor or two of homemade ice cream. Sit and enjoy the ambiance of the stunning courtyard cafe while you enjoy a scoop of refreshing ice cream in flavors like matcha or mint chocolate chip made with peppermint essential oil. Vegan options are often available!

Seahorse Republic

Stop by this funky little food truck located in Gallows Bay for PB & B (Peanut Butter and Banana) Ice Dream Sandwiches. The 'dream' part of their 'ice dream sandwiches' is, like everything else served at Seahorse, their desserts are vegan and gluten-free! Did I mention they are also scrumptious...even if you aren't vegan?

Shupe's on the Boardwalk

If you are looking for a casual stop at a waterfront bar that happens to offer ice cream, Shupe's is the place for you. Enjoy a beautiful view of Christiansted Harbor while you cool down with some vanilla softserve ice cream. There is something for everyone vanilla softserve ice cream cones for the kids, and adult milkshakes with your favorite liquor for the grown ups!

Deck Bar at Rum Runners

The Deck Bar at Rum Runners is a popular local hangout because it offers cold drinks on the go, and a very simple bar menu. They also offer an unobstructed view of Christiansted Harbor, and are home to the Christiansted webcam. What you may not know is that they also offer some of the most amazing ice cream sandwiches imaginable! Cool, refreshing ice cream sandwiched between two homemade cookies, these frozen treats are almost enough for two people to share...almost.

St. Croix is an island that lives in an eternal state of summer weather...so it's always a good time for ice cream! Remember, you can't buy happiness, but you can buy ice cream and that's kind of the same thing.

Christmas Time on St. Croix

While images of cerulean blue Caribbean waters and palm tree-lined beaches may not spring to mind when you think of Christmas, St. Croix is a wondrous place to spend the holidays. Starting the day after Thanksgiving, the holiday season is packed with events island wide where you can indulge in scrumptious local holiday foods and drinks, shop for locally made gifts, give to the St. Croix community, and celebrate Crucian Carnival. If you are planning a trip to St. Croix around the holidays, or even if you live here, take advantage of the many opportunities the island offers to get into the holiday spirit.

Christmas Jump Up has become the unofficial kick-off of the holiday events on St. Croix. While Jump Ups are held four times per year in Christiansted, Christmas Jump Up is the most anticipated of them all. This huge town-wide party includes live music, entertainment, shopping, local food vendors, and much more. Christmas Jump Up is also a great opportunity to see the island's iconic mocko jumbies and fire dancers perform, and local businesses stay open late so you can enjoy an evening of great dining and start your Christmas shopping too.

Starving Artist Day at Estate Whim offers the chance to shop the wares of local artists, photographers, jewelers, designers, craftspeople, and more. Find unique gifts that were handmade right here on St. Croix while enjoying aspects of Crucian culture like live music, dancing, and food in the historic setting of the Estate Whim Museum grounds.

Christmas Spoken Here is one of the great holiday traditions of St. Croix. As you meander around the grounds of the St. George Village Botanical Garden your senses will be delighted by the sounds of choirs singing, the delicious smell of barbecue, the taste of locally made coquito, and the sight of the spectacularly decorated Christmas trees in the Great Hall.

The St. Croix Christmas Boat Parade is a must-see for the holidays. Family-friendly events and entertainment start at noon on the Christiansted Boardwalk, but the main event happens when the boats parade through Christiansted Harbor decked in their holiday finest. Participating boats choose a theme and are decorated with thousands of lights, inflatables, and handmade decorations, some boats even have their own entertainment, DJ or musician on board! While prizes are awarded to the best boats in the show, the spectators are the real winners of this event. The parade is then followed by a spectacular fireworks display.

Gallows Bay Holiday Festival is an annual community event where you can take advantage of extended shopping hours at the stores in Gallows Bay while enjoying Christmas music, holiday treats, and live quadrille performances by the We Deh Yah Cultural Dancers. At this family-friendly event, children can also get their picture taken with Santa at Undercover Books & Gifts.

Holiday Fest in Frederiksted joins community and culture for a fun, family event. Sponsored by the VI Port Authority and the Frederiksted Economic Development Association, Holiday Fest includes live music, cultural dancers, steel pan orchestra performances, mocko jumbies, local majorettes, and arts and crafts vendors. This is kid friendly event which also features a Christmas tree lighting, visits with Santa Claus, and face painting for the kids.

Galas, benefits and fundraisers, oh my! With Christmas being a time for giving, there are also a number of wonderful charities and organizations here on St. Croix that host galas, benefits, and fundraisers in December. Holiday Hope is a benefit hosted by the St. Croix Hotel & Tourism Association and the St. Croix Chamber of Commerce to raise funds for the Boys & Girls Club of the Virgin Islands, CASA of the Virgin Islands, and the Richard Patrick Henry Scholarship Foundation. Holiday Hope features both a live and a silent auction, as well as complimentary hors d'oeuvers and live entertainment. The elegant Gala in the Garden is held at St. George Village Botanical Garden to benefit the Garden's education programs. Gala in the Garden includes a delicious holiday meal and a live auction.

If you prefer something more casual, The Blue Mutt holds a Holiday Cookie Sale each year at the December Art Thursday to raise money for the St. Croix Animal Welfare Center. You can donate by shopping the bake sale, providing three dozen cookies to be sold at the event, or you can volunteer your time to decorate, box cookies, or help out at the cookie sale.

Crucian Christmas Carnival events happen island wide all through December and into January, culminating with the Children and Adult Parades held the Friday and Saturday following Three Kings Day respectively. Carnival kicks-off with the opening of of the main Carnival Village in Frederiksted, and is followed by a series of cultural nights, soca competitions, pageantry, fairs, j'ouvert and more! The highlights of Carnival each year are the colorful Children and Adult Parades. As you stand along the parade route you are treated to the sight of troupes clad in vibrantly colored costumes dancing through the streets, along with themed parade floats, mocko jumbies, fire dancers and more. You will hear the sounds and feel the rhythms of steel pan orchestras, DJs and live musicians, and before you know it you will be dancing along.

Here on St. Croix, Christmas time provides the best of everything you could ask for this time of year. Not only do you get to enjoy warm weather and Caribbean beaches instead of snow, but you also get to see the island's community come together and truly celebrate the Christmas season. Crucian Christmas time reminds us to: appreciate the time we have with family and friends; give what we can to local charities and organizations; support local businesses and artisans; and, get out and enjoy the island paradise we call home. From all of us here at GoToStCroix.com, we wish you and your loved ones a safe and happy holiday season!

Find Your Park on St. Croix

The United States' National Park Service (NPS) is celebrating the centennial of their creation in 2016 with the "Find Your Park" program. Many Americans think of the Grand Canyon, Yellowstone or Yosemite when they think of national parks, but you can "Find Your Park" right here on St. Croix, USVI! While the island is only 82 square miles in size, St. Croix is home to three separate national parks: Buck Island Reef National Monument, Christiansted National Historic Site, and Salt River Bay National Historic Park and Ecological Preserve.

Buck Island Reef National Monument

Buck Island Reef is St. Croix's only underwater national park. In total, the park encompasses 176 acres above and below the water. It was established a National Monument by a Presidential proclamation in 1961, and grew in 2001 to preserve "one of the finest marine gardens in the Caribbean Sea." Above the water, Buck Island offers a hike along a nature trail to the highest peak for a breathtaking view. You can also stroll along the soft, white sand of Turtle Beach, who pristine condition makes it a popular filming location.

Below the water, enjoy an abundance of native marine flora a fauna, vibrant coral reefs, playful fish, friendly rays and the occasional endangered hawksbill turtle. Buck Island is home to an underwater trail off the east end of the island that is accessible mostly by full or half day snorkeling tours. Signs have been mounted underwater to indicate interesting structures, marine life habitats, and commonly seen fish species. Buck Island is accessible by boat only. There is no fee to access the island on a private boat, however fees do vary for full or half day snorkeling excursions depending on the tour operator.

Christiansted National Historic Site

Christiansted National Historic Site was first established on March 4, 1952, as Virgin Islands National Historic Site through the initiative of concerned local citizens, to preserve the historic structures and grounds within its boundaries, and to illustrate the Danish influence on the island between 1733 and 1917, including colonial administration, military and naval establishment, international trade (including slave trade), religious diversity, architecture, trades and crime and punishment, between 1733 and 1917.

The site was renamed to Christiansted National Historic Site on January 16, 1961 and was listed on the National Register of Historic Places on October 15, 1966. This 7 acre area park is located on the Christiansted waterfront and includes five historical structures: Fort Christiansvaern, the Scale House, the Danish Custom House, the Steeple Building, and the Danish West Indie & Guinea Company Warehouse. An informative walking tour is available at the visitor center at the park headquarters in the fort. Admission is $3 per person.

Salt River Bay National Historic Park and Ecological Preserve

Salt River is a 1,015 acre park not only important historically, but also as an ecological preserve. The NPS works jointly with the government to manage this park, which includes a prehistoric archaeological site, a visitors center, huge mangrove forests, a bioluminescent bay, and coral reefs. Salt River is also known as Columbus Landing since Christopher Columbus landed at this spot in America's Paradise in 1493. Columbus encountered the not-so-friendly Carib Indian tribe when landing, which led to the first documented conflict between Europeans and Native Americans. Some believe that Columbus never set foot on land, sending out a search party to explore the new land. Either way, we are proud of this beautiful area, which is recognized as a National Landmark.

According to the NPS: "The prehistoric complex at Salt River is one of the most important archaeological sites in the Virgin Islands. It has been the focus of every major archaeological investigation on St. Croix since 1880. Through artifact evidence and/or early historical accounts, we know that the area was inhabited by all three major pottery-making cultures found in the Virgin Islands in prehistoric times (Igneri, 50-650 AD; TAINO, 650-1450 AD; and Kalina or Carib, 1425-1590 AD). There is good reason to believe that the Salt River site was a major religious and cultural center as well as a long lived permanent settlement. The only Tainan ceremonial ball court or plaza (Batey) found so far in the Lesser Antilles was excavated there by a Danish archaeologist, Gudmund Hatt, in 1923. Artifacts associated with that game, including petroglyphs, stone "belts" (used either as trophies or handicaps), three-pointed stones called "zemis", and human sacrificial burials, are now in the possession of the National Museum in Copenhagen."

Salt River is no longer a fresh water supply, but is now a tropical ecosystem that supports threatened and endangered species. Salt

River Bay is home to one of the largest mangrove forests in the Virgin Islands as well as coral reefs and a submarine canyon. Salt River Bay is also one of only 7 year-round bioluminescent bays on Earth. Admission is free, but we recommend that you take advantage of the historical and ecological kayak tours to learn more about the area.

The National Park Service protects and serves national parks and local communities through it's programs. NPS is about state parks, local parks, trails, museums, historic sites, and the many ways that the American public can connect with history and culture, enjoy nature, and make new discoveries. Join in the celebration of the 100th birthday of the National Park Service by finding your park on St. Croix! Visit www.findyourpark.com to learn more, or to share your national park experience. To learn more about the national parks of St. Croix, you can download the free St. Croix National Park Service app. The app is available for download on both Apple and Android devices at iTunes and Google Play stores, it is entitled 'NPS-St. Croix, USVI (NPS-STX)' and includes information on all three of St. Croix's national parks. Have fun finding your park!

Fitness

Whether you are an athlete traveling to St. Croix for a competition, or just someone who wants to keep up your fitness routine, St. Croix has something for every age, budget and fitness level! Join us as we compile the many different fitness options to experience whether you are a walker, runner, swimmer, hiker, or into weight training, crossfit, yoga, zumba, cycling, and so much more.

The Final Ironman St. Croix 70.3 Triathlon

Many of our readers have asked why the Ironman St. Croix is coming to an end this year. We reached out to Race Director Tom Guthrie to get the official answer.

What started as the 'America's Paradise Triathlon' 29 years ago officially became the Ironman St. Croix 70.3 race in 2001 when it became a sanctioned Ironman course. The race became a popular one due to the beauty and difficulty of the course, known by triathletes as 'Beauty and the Beast', and the fact that the race offered qualifying spots for the Ironman World Championships race in Kailua-Kona. When the Ironman company moved the qualifying slots to another race, the number of participants began to steadily decline.

According to Tom, the growth of the Ironman franchise worldwide has given potential competitors more race options to choose from. When the St. Croix race began in 1988, there were less than 10 Ironman races in the world. Now, there are 200 Ironman races alone, three of which are scheduled on the same day as the St. Croix race. There was an Ironman in Puerto Rico six weeks ago, as well as a the Pro Championships the day before our race. Also, due to our remote location on St. Croix, we can no longer compete for the attendance when there are so many other races a person can choose from without the expense and distance of coming to St. Croix.

Tom is most proud of the track record of 28 previous races executed safely and efficiently, which defies the odds. Every Ironman race in the U.S. is run by a paid staff of 40 Ironman employees, while on St. Croix, the number of paid Ironman employees has always been ZERO. On St. Croix, this has been the people's race! There are 1,000 volunteers doing the work flawlessly, many of whom have volunteered every single year for the past 2+ decades. There is no paid staff. A few local businesses and individuals step up as sponsors, often with donated supplies. Several government agencies like the Police Department and the Department of Public Works have been incredible supporters of the event as well. We have 100% cooperation from so many key people and government offices that the race has endured for 28 years because of the people, and because it does NOT fit the mold.

Overall, St. Croix residents are sad that this is final year for the Ironman, but all good things must come to an end. It was Tom's decision to make 2017 the last year with Ironman wanting to finish on a positive note after a remarkable 29 year span. As most of us residents know, getting even simple tasks accomplished can be difficult at times, so it's quite incredible it has not only survived but thrived for as long as it has. According to Tom, if we approached Ironman about having a race on St. Croix now (as a new event), it would never be able to get off the ground. And yet, it has worked because of how unique it is, and because the community supported it.

We would like to express our sincere thanks to Race Director Tom Guthrie, along with the many volunteers, sponsors, participating government agencies, and the St. Croix community at large for making this event successful for so many years!

Where to Workout on St. Croix

Whether you are visiting St. Croix and you want to keep up your exercise routine, or you are a resident looking to mix-up your workouts, the island has a lot to offer. The variety and scope of fitness activities St. Croix has to offer is pleasantly surprising. From jogging trails with stunning views, to yoga classes in charming, courtyard studio spaces or on the sea, the island offers something for everyone and every fitness level!

Go for a jog or walk while enjoying some fresh ocean air. If you are in the Christiansted area, you can take advantage of the Christiansted

Bypass (a thoroughfare constructed to bypass the in-town traffic of Christiansted and connect the Orange Grove area to the Gallows Bay area). The bypass has a nice sidewalk that is about 1 1/2 miles long, is one big hill, and is one of the few even surfaces in Christiansted. The beauty is that as you walk or run the bypass, you overlook historic Christiansted and its harbor, the endless blue Caribbean Sea, and the colorful buildings of Gallows Bay. Limited free parking is available at the lookout point near the top of the bypass, or in Christiansted at either end of the bypass.

If you are heading towards the East End, you can stop into The Buccaneer and use their jogging trail which offers breathtaking views of the turquoise water, and their lush resort and golf course. This meandering two-mile trail offers both flat areas and hills, and is interspersed with workout stations, so it is a great option for any fitness level. The entrance to the trail is outside and to the left of the resort entrance gate, and can be accessed in the early morning and late afternoon hours. Free parking is available in the parking lot just outside of the resort entrance near the trail access, but please be aware of the golfers. The jogging trail runs along the golf course and the golfers have the right-of-way, so please pay attention and be courteous.

Go for a scenic bike ride. For those that prefer a bike workout, the East End of St. Croix offers the East End Loop. This 13 mile bicycle route is comprised of the loop made by South Shore Road, East End Road, and their connection point ('Pelican Way') on the easternmost point in the loop. This scenic ride takes cyclers along St. Croix's beautiful North Shore and South Shores, countless picturesque bays, and includes views of the iconic Contessa's Castle and the Divi Carina Bay Resort and Casino. Or, for those who seek a little more adventure, the rainforest offers some great mountain biking. For your safety, please be mindful the road conditions, watch for potholes and traffic as you ride along the road.

Utilize the Frederiksted Pier in any way you can! The pier is open to the public (except on days there is a cruise ship in port) so you can walk, run, bike or even rollerblade your way up and down the 1,500+ foot pier for an energizing workout. Even better, you can cool off after your workout by jumping off the pier! There is a designated area that is accessible to the public and has a ladder to help you get back up. In this area jump is about 25 feet, and the water is just as deep. Since ocean conditions are usually flat and calm in this area, you can also take advantage of some of the island's best swimming, snorkeling and stand-up paddle boarding. But, be aware that there is no lifeguard or rescue boat, so please be safe! Parking for the pier is located along the waterfront Strand Street and along Frederiksted Beach on the north side of Fort Frederik.

Get your 'om' on with a yoga or fitness class. There are a multitude of yoga and fitness classes available island wide, in some amazing settings. In Christiansted you can choose from a huge variety of classes 6 days a week in the serene surroundings of The Courtyard Juices & Fitness Studio. The Courtyard can provide yoga mats, and they offer both drop-in rates and multi-class cards, whichever best suits your needs. Classes at The Courtyard range from yoga and dance, to hoop and flow. Or, take your yoga practice at sea level, abroad Lyric Sails' 63ft 'Jolly Mon' sailing catamaran. Let tranquility wash over you as Lyric Sails secures the boat and for an hour of yoga with a certified instructor on deck atop the Caribbean Sea, followed by a complimentary healthy drink and an hour guided meditation cruise along St. Croix's picturesque West End before returning to port.

You can also now enjoy SUP yoga and fitness classes on the East End of St. Croix at Chenay Bay with Stone Bodyworks Wellness. These classes explore simple yoga poses while you are on a stand-up paddleboard. Learn yoga poses while adapting to the motion of the board, challenge yourself to balance any instability created by minor energy and weight shifts, and learn to focus and ground yourself while afloat.

Hit the gym. St. Croix offers a traditional gym, as well as the well known 340 CrossFit gym both of which offer passes to accommodate the amount of time you will be spending on the island. You can also hire a personal trainer, or try a new fitness class like Zumba, Barre, Bootcamp, or even Water Aerobics. If you are visiting the island, many of the resorts and hotels now have fitness centers available to their guests. Make sure to ask what fitness activities your resort or hotel has available for your use while you enjoy your time on St. Croix!

Find a pickup game. All around St. Croix you can find groups playing a variety of different pickup games pretty regularly. You can find traditional pickup games like basketball, soccer, and softball being played at sports complexes and recreation centers island wide. Or, you can try something a little more unique like kickball. Several of St. Croix's beaches, including Rainbow Beach and Tamarind Reef, offer beach volleyball games on the weekends.

Go for a swim in the Caribbean. Last, but definitely not least, St. Croix has an abundance of warm, clear Caribbean water available on any shore island wide...so, go for a swim! Not only is it great exercise, but salt water is good for the soul!

While you can certainly get your exercise by enjoying some of the island's popular outdoor activities such as hiking, golfing, snorkeling, diving, kayaking, or stand-up paddle boarding, you can also stick to a more traditional workout. No matter what your age, fitness level, or length of time you will be on the island, St. Croix offers a fitness option for EVERYONE, so take advantage!

Achieve Balance at a Yoga Class

Yoga is practiced worldwide by millions of people, and offers some incredible health and wellness benefits. The beauty of yoga is that can be practiced almost anywhere, and by anyone. Here on St. Croix, there is a thriving yoga community and classes are offered island wide for every level of yoga practitioner. Take advantage of some of the yoga classes offered on this beautiful island to achieve balance for yourself, and to refresh your body, mind and soul.

If you are not yet familiar with yoga, it combines poses (or postures) and movement, breathing exercises, relaxation, self-awareness and meditation in order to cultivate physical, mental and emotional health and well-being. Probably the most well known aspect of yoga is balance. On a physical level, practicing yoga strengthens and tones your core muscles, which in turn improves your balance but, yoga offers mental and emotional balance in addition to the physical. Yoga teaches you to let go of stress, relax your body, breathe deeply, and look inward to find peace and happiness. Flexibility is another well know component of yoga. If you think you're not flexible enough to start doing yoga, relax. You will find that flexibility is a result of practicing yoga, regardless of how flexible you are to begin with. The flexibility and balance you gain from yoga will also be accompanied by increased strength and coordination, enhanced cardiovascular health, and a sense of overall well-being.

Yoga offers some amazing benefits, even if you only practice for one hour a week. Some of the more well documented benefits of practicing yoga include:

- ✓ Increased balance, endurance, strength and flexibility
- ✓ Reduced stress and physical tension, which leads to increased memory and self-awareness
- ✓ Increased emotional health, and decreased depression and anxiety
- ✓ Strengthening of the spine and core muscles, providing relief from back pain
- ✓ Improved posture
- ✓ Reduced risk of heart disease and arthritis
- ✓ Improved sleep

If you have never taken a class before, don't be intimidated. In general, instructors are friendly and are willing to help you get started and make sure you get the poses correct as you go through the class.

To get started you really only need comfortable clothing and a yoga mat. Wear comfortable, stretchy clothing that does not impede your movement so that you to stretch every which way, hold the poses, and move easily between poses. Yoga is generally done on an aptly named 'yoga mat'. These mats are designed to provide traction for some of the standing poses, as well as a little bit of cushion for those poses that involve sitting or lying down on the floor. You can buy a yoga mat at most yoga studios, gyms, department or sporting goods stores, or online. If you don't own one, or aren't ready to buy one just yet, you can often borrow them from the the studio or gym where you are taking your yoga class.

To pick the right class to get started, you will want to read the class descriptions or ask your local studio or instructor which class is right for a beginner. If you are a more advanced yoga practitioner, consider trying a new type of yoga to challenge yourself. Here on St. Croix you can try: Ashtanga (a more vigorous style of yoga offering a series of poses, each held for only five breaths), Vinyasa (classes that flow from one pose to the next without stopping to talk about the finer points of each pose), Hatha (a gentle yoga class), Kemetic (a healing and regenerative Yoga system that is characterized by a series of geometrically progressive postures that creates alignment of the spinal column and corrects defects in the skeletal muscular system), or

Fundamentals of Yoga (a great beginner class). There are even yoga classes offered here on the island for children and teens.

If you want to step outside the box of standard yoga classes, consider doing yoga on the water. Enjoy the beautiful waters or the Caribbean while you strike your poses. Lyric Sails offers yoga classes aboard their catamaran on the calm waters of St. Croix's West End. If you want to take things to the next level, try yoga on a stand up paddleboard as part of a SUP Fitness class, currently being offered at Chenay Bay.

No matter what your experience level, yoga will help you to achieve and maintain a harmonious balance between your physical, emotional, and mental self, and will promote general well-being in many aspects of your life. St. Croix offers some beautiful courtyard studios, yoga on the beach, a yoga and meditation sail, and yoga retreats to nourish your body and soul. You can even find one-on-one wellness coaches through EvolveVI Movement or Stone Bodyworks Wellness that can teach you the basics of breathing and movement to ease you into yoga safely.

Enter a Road Race

Many think of St. Croix as a tropical paradise full of beaches, where people spend their days basking in the sun and floating in the Caribbean Sea. While that is partially true, there is also a huge fitness and running community here on the island. For visitors and residents, this means that while you enjoy this slice of paradise, you can also enter one (or more) of dozens of different road races offered on St. Croix each year. No matter what your current fitness level, there is a race for you.

Here on St. Croix, the Virgin Islands Pace Runners coordinate dozens of races annually for adults, kids, families, and athletes. From 520 meter runs to ultra marathons, there is something for adults and children of all ages. If you are just getting started, or you will be walking the event instead of running, I would recommend trying a 5K (which is 3.1 miles). Some of the more well known annual 5K road races include the Veterans Day 5K, the Paradise 5K, and the National Library Week Run to Your Library 5K. Or, try aiming a little higher with the The Flight #64 Four Mile or join in the fun of the Cane Bay 5 Mile. If you have never tried a road race before and are intimated by the idea of a 5K, consider doing one of the even shorter races such as the Three Kings Mile, the Memorial Day 2 Mile, the Olympic Day Run (1 mile), or the Women's Race (2 miles).

First time racer? Don't worry! As someone who is not a runner, but has completed many 5K and 4.12 mile races, and even a half marathon, I can tell you anything is possible! Don't let the term 'race' scare you, you are a winner just for participating. In fact, even though I usually set a reasonable time goal for myself, my true goal is always simply to finish the race. To get you started, here are a few tips to make your first 5K more comfortable, and maybe even enjoyable:

1. **Get to the race early.** Make sure you read the emails and handouts provided by the race organization to let you know the details of the races, including transportation, start times, parking, and street closures on race morning.

2. **Wear comfortable clothing and shoes.** A 5K can be a LONG race if your feet hurt, or your clothes are rubbing or chaffing. Make sure you wear clothes and tennis shoes you know are comfortable, and that you have run or walked in prior to race day.

3. **Keep your pace steady.** It's a good to know your average mile pace so that you know if you are going too fast or slow during the race, then you can adjust accordingly. You don't want to start out too fast and burn out too soon.

4. **Focus on yourself and your race.** Sometimes when you get to a race it can be overwhelming and there can be a lot of action, noise and stuff going on. Take time before the race starts to w

arm up, sip some water, find your starting area/corral, and set your personal goals or intentions for the race.

5. **Live in the moment.** It's your first 5K! It should be empowering to do something that you've never done before, or that you didn't think was possible. Enjoy the race route and the overall experience.

6. **Recruit your friends and family.** You will often see groups dressed in the same t-shirt getting ready to run and supporting each other the whole way, which makes the experience more fun. You can definitely run alone if you choose, but signing up with a partner or group of others creates more accountability and a 'we're-in-this-together' mentality.

Don't forget about the kids! Many children love to run just for fun, and really enjoy getting to participate in a race. There are a few special race events held for kids including the Children's Race (800 meters) and the Children Run Christiansted (520 meters). Even as a spectator, these are fun races. The parents, friends and community come out and cheer on all of the racers. Plus, the kids all receive medals or ribbons for participating. Make race day a family affair by participating with your little ones, or by being supportive and encouraging to your kids.

For the more serious athletes out there (or those looking for more of a challenge than a 5K), St. Croix offers a beautiful, but challenging race environment for a wide range of distance races. For the true endurance runner, the St. Croix Scenic 50 Ultra Marathon offers stunning views as you traverse 50 miles of the island's historic towns, mountains, rainforest, and shoreline. Not quite ready for 50 miles? Consider participating in the St. Croix International Marathon (26.2 miles) or Half Marathon (13.1 miles). You can also take in both of the historic towns of Christiansted and Frederiksted, and everything in between, by participating in the annual Martin Luther King Fort-to-Fort Run (15.5 miles).

Take a Fitness Class on St. Croix

Looking to change up your fitness routine? St. Croix offers a variety of different fitness classes for all ages and fitness levels. From high-intensity CrossFit classes, to flexibility increasing barre classes, there is something for everyone. Try a new type fitness class to get yourself inspired to get back into shape, or mix in a new type of class to vary your existing fitness regimen. Here at GoToStCroix.com, we have found several different classes here on the island that are taking the world by storm, so you may want to give them a try.

I'm sure by now, if you haven't already tried it, you have at least heard of CrossFit. The general goal of CrossFit is to improve physical fitness, athletic performance, and quality of life as a whole. CrossFit uses functional exercises to optimize each individual's physical competence in all ten of the recognized fitness categories: cardiovascular and respiratory endurance, stamina, strength, flexibility, power, speed, coordination, agility, balance, and accuracy. So, what can you expect when you visit a CrossFit gym? First, you will not find machines, you will instead see varieties of free weights, pull up bars, ropes, tires, huge boxes, and more. These fitness tools are utilized by CrossFitters during the 'workout of the day' (or WOD). CrossFit gyms place proper technique and consistency before intensity, so that your WOD is performed safely and efficiently for maximum results. Here is a great video that explains what CrossFit is and what you can expect:

The good news about CrossFit is that the WODs can be tailored for any fitness level or to address an injury. If a particular exercise is not immediately possible, in nearly every case there is a method to reduce the load to insignificant levels while maintaining the line of action that will prepare you for the missing capacity as your strength increases. For example, weightlifting exercise can be done with a broomstick or PVC pipe if a weight is too heavy. Not being able to complete a WOD doesn't mean that you can't do CrossFit. Taking a WOD and reducing the load, cutting the reps, dropping a set, taking longer rests, and/or sitting down a few times during the workout is still doing CrossFit, you are just turning down the intensity.

On St. Croix, 340 CrossFit promotes mindfulness and respect in their gym (or 'box'). Positivity, motivation, inspiration, respect, teaching, learning, completion of assignments, focus on precision, honesty and intensity make up 340 CrossFit. They offer a fitness community where members and visitors are inspired by each other, and feel welcome. 340 CrossFit offers an atmosphere that is always positive, respectful and encouraging. You will often hear other members cheering you on and you will find yourself doing the same to others. In addition to a regular schedule of CrossFit classes, 340 CrossFit offers team workouts and kids CrossFit, so the whole family can get fit together. If you want to give it a try, 340 CrossFit offers monthly and yearly unlimited membership options, and class pass options for those coming less frequently. They also encourage locals to come and try a complimentary introductory class, and welcome visitors to drop in while here on vacation!

Looking for a fun way to get some fitness in that feels like play? Try a Hoop Radiance class. In Hoop Radiance all levels of students are welcome and you will learn the basics of hula hooping while strengthening your core and aligning your body.

If you are looking for a way to get a great workout while getting in some stretching (and a little Zen time), you may want to consider taking a barre class. Barre classes use a combination of postures inspired by ballet, yoga and Pilates. The barre is used as a prop to balance while doing exercises that focus on isometric strength training (holding your body still while you contract a specific set of muscles) combined with high reps of small range-of-motion movements. Barre classes also often incorporate light handheld weights to increase the burn during all those reps, as well as using yoga mats for targeted core work. The beauty of barre classes are the benefits which include weight loss, improved posture, increased muscle definition, increased flexibility and reduced stress. Barre classes are great for just about any fitness level because the technique was designed so that the positions and movements are basic, it's how deep you work in them that makes the difference in the intensity.

Looking for a fun, fast-paced workout? Zumba would be a great option for you! Zumba is essentially a Latin-inspired cardio-dance workout that uses music and choreographed steps to form a fitness party atmosphere. While many of the types of dance and music featured in the program are Latin American inspired, classes can also contain everything from jazz to African beats to country to hip-hop and pop. Zumba is known for taking the 'work' out of workout by mixing low-intensity and high-intensity moves in an interval-style, calorie-burning 'dance fitness party'. Zumba classes offer a total body workout, combining all the major elements of fitness: cardio, muscle conditioning, balance and flexibility. According to their website, Zumba also offers: 'boosted energy and a serious dose of awesome each time you leave class'. How can you go wrong with a workout that feels like a fun dance party rather than a fitness class?

Zumba is truly a workout for anyone who can stand up and dance and I use the term 'dance' very loosely. No dance experience or skills are necessary. People of all ages, shapes and sizes are welcome and encouraged to attend classes. So, what can you expect from a Zumba class? Most Zumba classes are about an hour long, beginning with a dynamic warm-up and ending with a cool down and some static stretching. The workout itself is broken down by song, each with a different choreographed dance routine.

Unlike other aerobics classes, where you learn a move and then add on more moves to create a routine, Zumba uses different parts of the songs as the basis of its choreography. Zumba is also unique in that its instructors don't speak very much. Instead they cue you on what to do with hand signals of which direction to move, or a loud hand clap that signifies that it's time to move to a new move. Overall, participants learn as they go through repetition and by example. This can be frustrating for first-timers, but don't fret...Zumba uses a lot of the same songs over and over, you will get the hang of it after a few classes. Here on the island, you can even take Zumba in the pool, so you can keep cool while you dance your way to fitness!

If you enjoy the water, a SUP Fitness class may be just the thing for you. SUP Fitness combines movement and strengthening exercises on the beach with some stand up paddleboarding and stretching. This is a fun and unique way to enjoy a group class on the beach, and on the water.

In addition to the classes described above, you can find some of the more traditional or well known fitness classes like Pilates, spinning, body sculpting, yoga, kickboxing, and water aerobics. There is a fitness class for everyone out there, you just have to find the one that fits you. Remember to dress appropriately for the classes you choose, and drink plenty of water before and after to stay hydrated. I recommend taking a friend with you to make the experience more fun, and so that you have someone to help you keep up your fitness routine and stay motivated. Most importantly, enjoy the feeling of accomplishment that comes after completing a great workout. You've earned it!

Golf in Paradise

If you want to golf in paradise, St. Croix offers some of the best courses in the Caribbean. Don't miss your opportunity to play one of the island's picturesque courses which have been written about in publications like Golf Digest, Travel and Leisure Golf, and GOLF magazine. Choose a golf course in a lush valley surrounded by rainforest, a scenic resort course overlooking the turquoise Caribbean Sea, or a 9-hole course set amongst swaying palm trees and the tranquil breezes of St. Croix's East End. (Or, better yet, try all three!)

Whether you are a pro or a leisure golfer, or you have never swung a club in your life, there is a golf course for every skill level here on St. Croix. Golf 9 or 18 holes, hit a bucket of balls at one of two driving ranges, hone your skills on the practice putting green, take golf lessons, peruse the pro shops, and much more. While you are here in America's Paradise, indulge in a game of golf and take advantage of the warm weather of an endless summer and the beautiful landscapes of St. Croix and the surrounding Caribbean Sea.

Go for a Run or Walk

There are many areas here on St. Croix to go for a run or, if your more my speed, a walk. If you are going to get some exercise, you might as well enjoy the fresh ocean air, the year-round summer climate, and the scenic views.

Whether you are a resident looking for a new route, or a visitor looking to keep up your fitness routine, we have compiled a list of routes for you to consider.

Christiansted...

Christiansted Bypass (Route 66): About one and a half miles long, the bypass is a large hill offering a nice sidewalk and some parking on each end. This route offers great views of Christiansted Harbor and Gallows Bay.

Estate Hermon Hill Road: Off of Route 83 this road leads through the Hermon Hill neighborhood, over rolling hills. The road is about one mile long and paved, but no sidewalks.

East End...

Jogging Trail at The Buccaneer: A meandering three mile trail offering both flat areas and hills, offering amazing views of The Buccaneer golf course and the Caribbean Sea. Free parking is available in the parking lot just outside of the resort entrance near the trail access.

Cramer's Park to Point Udall: A nice, even, paved road, about one and a half miles long from Cramer's Park to Point Udall. There is plenty of parking at Cramer's Park, but you will have to run on the street since there is no sidewalk.

South Shore Road: A relatively straight four mile stretch of road between Grapetree Bay and Great Pond. There is no sidewalk, but the road is paved and the view of the South Shore and the sea is breathtaking.

Neighborhood Roads: There are several major neighborhood roads that wind through the East End quarters, such as Seven Flags Road or Tipperary Road, which offer paved (or partially paved) roads.

Chenay Bay Beach to Green Cay Marina: If you are looking for a great beach run (or walk) park at the Chenay Bay and walk to the end of the beach at Green Cay Marina. This route is just over half a mile each way, but you get great resistance from the sand.

North Shore...

North Shore Road (Cane Bay to Carambola Beach Resort): A mile and a half each way, this route offers amazing North Shore ocean views, and areas shaded by subtropical rainforest. You can park at Cane Bay beach, or just outside of the Carambola Beach Resort.

The Beast (Route 69): This well known hill starts at North Shore Road and winds uphill to the Carambola Golf Course. A well known feature of the St. Croix Ironman Triathlon, The Beast is a 600 foot uphill 'climb' in a stretch of highway about three-quarters of a mile long with a steep grade.

West End...

Frederiksted Pier: Run or speed walk your way down to the end of the pier and back for an energizing workout. The pier is only about one-third of a mile long (so if you are in good shape you might need to do a few 'laps'), but the view of the island's picturesque West End is stunning.

Route 63: Head along Route 63 going north out of Frederiksted. This is a relatively straight mile and a half long stretch of road, along the shore of the West End along Frederiksted Beach and Rainbow Beach. There is no sidewalk, but the road is paved; however, you do need to watch for potholes.

No matter where you choose to run or walk, please keep your personal health and safety in mind. Here are a few things for your consideration:

- ✓ Take plenty of water with you and stay hydrated.
- ✓ The sun us very intense on St. Croix, so be sure to wear sunblock and/or other sun protection.
- ✓ The roads here on the island are narrow and curvy in areas which can make it difficult for drivers to see you, so please be aware of surrounding cars.

✓ Many of the roads have potholes, loose gravel, or uneven surfaces, so watch where you are running and wear proper shoes.

✓ If you are going to park your vehicle and leave it to go for a run, do not leave valuables in your vehicle.

Enjoy your time on the island (even your exercise), and consider taking a dip in the Caribbean Sea to cool off when your done with your run!

Food and Drink

For those of you that believe variety is the spice of life, you can find many different kinds of cuisine on St. Croix American fare, Caribbean, Latin and European foods and more. If you like fresh seafood, we recommend you try the locally caught spiny lobster, wahoo or mahi mahi (also called dolphin fish). If you like a little adventure with your food and spirits, try attending a farm to table dinner and plan to visit St. Croix in April during the St. Croix Food & Wine Experience, a weeklong celebration. Good food and drinks make for a great experience. Bringing you restaurant suggestions, great meals we've enjoyed, and island inspired recipes straight from the St. Croix food scene.

The Marvelous Mango

Mangoes are the most widely consumed fruit in the world, but besides their coveted flavor and sweetness, they also offer a ton of nutritional benefits. St. Croix is one of the best places on earth to be during mango season. In late June and early July the island is dripping with dozens of varieties of the delicious fruit.

Aside from the mango trees you can find seemingly everywhere, you will find local mangoes for sale at farm stands, on restaurant menus, and sometimes even set out for the public to take for free. St. Croix is even home to an annual event known throughout the Caribbean called Mango Melee, held at St. George Village Botanical Garden, which is centered around the fruit and it's many uses.

Health Benefits

Packed with vitamins, minerals, phytonutrients, and fiber, this sweet and delicious fruit offers a number of health benefits. Here are just 10 of the many benefits of the marvelous mango:

1. **Prevents Cancer:** Research has shown that the antioxidant compounds in mangoes have been found to protect against several different kinds of cancers, most effectively colon and breast cancers.

2. **Lowers Cholesterol:** The high levels of fiber, pectin and vitamin C help to lower cholesterol levels, especially Low-Density Lipoprotein (LDL), the bad kind.

3. **Boosts Immunity:** The generous amounts of vitamin C, vitamin A, and 20+ different types of carotenoids help keep your immune system healthy and strong.

4. **Prevents Asthma:** The risks for developing asthma are lower in people who consume a high amount of beta-carotene, the nutrient found in mangoes that gives them their orange color.

5. **Prevents Heart Disease:** The fiber, potassium, and vitamin content in mangoes all help to ward off heart disease. In fact, an increase in potassium intake coupled with a decrease in sodium intake is the most effective dietary change a person can make to reduce their risk of heart disease.

6. **Improves Digestion:** Like papayas, mangoes also contain enzymes that break down protein. Plus, the fiber in mangoes helps aid in digestion and elimination.

7. **Improves Skin and Hair Health:** Mangoes are great for your hair and skin because they are high in vitamin A. Vitamin A is a nutrient required for sebum production, which keeps hair

moisturized, and vitamin A is also necessary for the growth of all bodily tissues, including skin and hair. Additionally, adequate intake of vitamin C is needed for the building and maintaining of collagen, which provides structure to skin and hair. Mangoes can also be used both internally and externally for the skin to help clear clogged pores and eliminate pimples.

8. **Improves Eye Health:** Just one cup of sliced mangoes supplies 25% of the needed daily value of vitamin A, which promotes good eyesight as well as preventing night blindness and dry eyes.

9. **Controls Blood Sugar:** Blood sugar spikes and drops are common in people who are overweight, and these spikes and drops can lead to insulin resistance and metabolic syndrome, which affects the development of diabetes. Choosing sweet mango instead of other sugary treats can help control blood sugar, which then regulates insulin levels and reduces the risk of developing these other diseases.

10. **Helps Boost Metabolism:** The fiber in mangoes is excellent at fueling the probiotic bacteria that live in your gut, which aid in the absorption of certain vitamins, such as B12, which is needed for good energy metabolism.

Selecting, Peeling and Cutting Mangoes

St. Croix's local farmer's markets and farm stands, like ARTfarm, offer many varieties of locally grown mangoes for your noshing pleasure. If you are not familiar with purchasing fresh mangoes, here are a few tips for selecting the best fruit, and ripening it if necessary:

- ✓ Don't judge a mango by its color red does not not mean ripe (in fact, red can mean the fruit is overripe)

- ✓ Squeeze the mango gently to judge ripeness a ripe mango will "give" slightly, but will not be soft or squishy

- ✓ A firm mango will ripen at room temperature over a few days, but you can speed up ripening by placing firm mangoes in a paper bag at room temperature

- ✓ Once ripe, mangoes can be moved to the refrigerator to slow down ripening for several days

Now that you have picked out your mangoes, how do you cut them up? If you have never actually peeled and cut up a mango, or if you struggle to do so, here is a great video tutorial that shows one of the easiest ways:

Recipes:

There are few things on earth as delicious and sweet as a ripe mango...so enjoy the fruit by itself, blend it into smoothies, mix it into yogurt, use it a s a topping for everything from vanilla ice cream to salads, make it into salsa, bake it into cakes, or concoct a refreshing tropical cocktail with it. In fact, here are a couple of great mango and rum recipes from the local Cruzan Rum and Captain Morgan Rum distilleries:

Now that you know all the amazing health benefits of mangoes, and you are an expert and picking them out and prepping them, you can dig in! However you like to enjoy your mangoes, savor the flavor knowing that you are not just treating your taste buds, you are nourishing your entire body.

Reef Responsible Promotes Local Sustainability

For those who may not know, St. Croix's culinary scene is exploding! 2017 kicked off with an eight page spread called "Eating St. Croix" in Coastal Living magazine, and two of the island's restaurants, balter and Savant, made the list of USA Today's 10 Best Restaurants in the Caribbean. With a spotlight being shone on St. Croix's food scene, and with limited local resources available on an island, restaurants are focusing now more than ever on sustainability. Enter the Reef Responsible program, spearheaded by The Nature Conservancy's Coral Conservation Manager, Kemit Amon-Lewis.

Born and raised here on the of St. Croix, Kemit has a passion for preserving the beautiful reefs and marine ecosystem of St. Croix, the Caribbean, and the world for that matter. Kemit started the Reef

Responsible program back in 2014 right here on St. Croix as a collaboration between like-minded agencies including: The Nature Conservancy, NOAA's USVI Fisheries Liaison, the USVI Department of Planning and Natural Resources Division of Fish and Wildlife, University of the Virgin Islands, and St. Croix Reef Jam, and was funded by The Nature Conservancy and NOAA's Coral Reef Conservation Program. The program has been so successful on St. Croix that Kemit is now being "nudged" by the USVI Department of Tourism to expand the program to St. Thomas, St. John, and Puerto Rico.

So what does being "Reef Responsible" mean, and why is it so important? Being "Reef Responsible" comes down to using marine natural resources responsibly so that we don't deplete or harm those natural resources. The Caribbean has historically harvested reef fishes as a major food source, but the advancement of fishing gear and other technologies has caused reefs to be over-fished. Reef fishes are extremely important to the health of coral reefs, especially the herbivorous fish, like parrotfish and tangs, because they remove algae from the reefs which provides space for corals to settle and grow. Excessive removal of these critical fish species, along with other threats, have lead to a decline in the Caribbean coral reefs and the entire marine ecosystem. The Reef Responsible program was created to help combat over-fishing and promote the health of our coral reefs.

The mission of Reef Responsible is to increase the public's understanding of how catching, purchasing, serving and consuming locally harvested seafood can positively influence the future of the USVIs' commercial fishing and coral reefs.

Once the basic principals for the Reef Responsible program had been established, the Reef Responsible Sustainable Seafood Initiative was started. The Sustainable Seafood Initiative is a voluntary program designed to help create a sustainable seafood industry in the USVI by celebrating and recognizing those restaurants that are committed to supporting local fishers, and making conscious decisions about the seafood that they purchase, prepare, and serve. Through this initiative, training is provided to local restaurant owners and chefs toward improved practices regarding the purchase of seafood to be used in their restaurants. Information on seasonal closures and size restrictions for reef fishes, lobster, whelk, and conch is also provided in an effort to improve compliance with local and federal fisheries regulations. For example, "Good Choice" fishes are open-water or pelagic species such as dolphinfish, wahoo, and tuna as well as the non-native lionfish, an invasive species currently threatening the reef fish population. The restaurants that commit to the Sustainable Seafood Initiative are promoted by Reef Responsible on the Reef

Connect website, through the Reef Responsible Facebook page, and throughout the year at events such as Taste of St. Croix and Dine VI.

With sustainability coming to the forefront of the global environmental stage, Reef Responsible has plans to expand their program to to include supermarkets and fishers. Through the Sustainable Seafood Initiative, Reef Responsible continues to highlight those restaurants, and eventually will highlight those supermarkets and fishers, that make commitments to sustainable seafood practices. You can do your part by choosing to frequent the restaurants that are Reef Responsible.

Sample Locally Made Brews

For the past few years, microbrews and craft beers have been taking America by storm. The makers of these small-batch brews are generally recognized for their emphasis on quality, flavor and traditional brewing technique. While St. Croix may be an island, you can still find some refreshing, locally made ales and craft brews right in the heart of downtown Christiansted at The Bombay Club.

For the past 30 years, The Bombay Club has been a favorite haunt of residents and visitors alike. Known for offering consistently great food at reasonable prices, Bombay has recently embraced the concept of serving locally crafted beer as well. A seemingly fitting place to find craft brews, this quaint and unassuming restaurant and bar are housed in a historical Danish brick building tucked back in a small courtyard off of King Street. If you have never been, you really have to watch for the small wooden sign hanging street side which reads simply "The Bombay Club", under which you will usually find a specials board. When you enter the courtyard, a green awning marks the cavernous arched stone entryway into the restaurant. Once inside, the air conditioned comfort and casual vibe invite you to sit at the bar and grab a cold one.

So what exactly makes a craft brew (or microbrew) special? Turns out, there is an "official" Brewer's Association that has defined what it means to be a craft brewer. Essentially, it is a small, independently owned and operated brewery that uses traditional brewing methods. I can imagine just how "small" and "independent" our local island brewer is, so I think it's safe to consider him a craft brewer. The Bombay Club currently offers two different locally crafted beers on draft. Bombay Pale Ale is the house draft and is therefore (almost) always available on tap. The second type of beer on tap rotates depending on what the brewer has made, which was a stout the last time I was there.

If you are looking for a reason to choose a craft beer over a mass produced one, just consider the challenges craft brewers face -

especially those trying to brew beer here on St. Croix. Access to and the cost of raw materials and ingredients, access to and cost of fresh water, operational costs, and finding a market for the finished product are some of the bigger hurdles our local brewers have to overcome. So, keep in mind that when you order locally crafted beer you are not only supporting the community and culture of craft brewing in the United States, but you are also supporting our local island economy.

Raise your glass, take a sip, and savor the creativity and passion shown by our local brewer. Enjoy the complexity of the flavors and ingredients in your beer as you celebrate the fact that you are partaking of this delicious fermented beverage on a beautiful island in the Caribbean. Cheers!

Dine VI

Each year, the U.S. Virgin Island's showcases our cuisine and island culture with our own version of Restaurant Week: Dine VI. Enjoy great food, rum and wine tastings, live music, and historical tours as St. Croix celebrates our local flavors. This culinary celebration of the cuisine, culture and community of St. Croix features an array of events and dining experiences, in addition to the traditional three-course prix fixe menu offerings found at other Restaurant Weeks.

Dine VI Events

The USVI Department of Tourism is currently planning the events for the 2016 Dine VI, but here is a list of the events that were included in the 2015 inaugural Dine VI:

Friends of James Beard Foundation Benefit Dinner (Thursday, October 20th): The James Beard Foundation's mission is to celebrate, nurture, and honor America's diverse culinary heritage through programs that educate and inspire. The Benefit Dinner will be held at Balter in downtown in Christiansted, dinner will be prepared by Host Chef Digby Stridiron and Guest Chef Jose Enrique.

Food Learn (Thursday, October 27th, from 12:00PM 2:00PM): The Virgin Islands Good Food Coalition is excited to collaborate with the Virgin Islands Department of Tourism, Department of Agriculture, Landmark Society, Ridge to Reef Farm and other partners on the 2nd Annual Dine VI FOOD LEARN project. A stellar opportunity to expose youth, teachers and community stakeholders to locally sourced, produce and Farm and Food Education. The event is being held at the Estate Whim Museum.

Frederiksted Waterfront Entertainment and Food Truck Festival (Friday, October 28th, from 5:00pm 11:00pm): Come taste some of the best food truck eats on the island! The Frederiksted Economic

Development Association is proud to present "The Food Truck Festival on the Frederiksted Waterfront", featuring leading Virgin Islands Musical Sensation, Spectrum Band, Tia, DJ Swain and First Class Sounds. The event is taking place at the Verne I. Richards Veterans Memorial Park at the Frederiksted Waterfront.

Sejah Farms Chef Cookoff (Saturday, October 29th, from 7:00am 5:00pm): Come participate and see only VI locally grown foods at Sejah Farm Famers' Market Stand and featuring local produce prepared by some of the top chefs and local cooks on Island. This event is based on the creativity of the participating cooks and chefs. "Bush Cook" chefs would choose to us a coal pot, three stone setting, a hole in the ground or whatever bush style cooking they like.

Reef Responsible Fish Fry (Sunday, October 30th, from 11:00am 6:00pm): Come and experience a delicious array reef responsible seafood dishes and musical performance by Romanza. See Food Sustainably at Fort Frederik.

Feast Christiansted (Saturday, November 5, from 5:30pm 10:00pm): A night of entertainment and fine dining experiences in Historic Christiansted, produced in partnership with the Christiansted Restaurant and Retail Association. The streets come alive with strolling musicians, and discount coupons are available for over 30 participating shops and restaurants! Print your coupons here: DineVI_2016-FeastCsted-flyer

Participating Restaurants

During the Dine VI event, participating restaurants will offer special three-course lunch and dinner, so taste your way through St. Croix and enjoy a variety of appetizers, entreés, and desserts. Take advantage of this special event to try some new island restaurants and return to your favorites. Each participating restaurant will offer amazing prix-fixe menus at a special price of $35 or $49. Here is a list of the participating restaurants for 2016:

RESTAURANT	PRICE	PHONE
2 Plus 2 Restaurant	Lunch ($15)	(340) 718-3710
40 Strand Eatery	Lunch ($20), Dinner ($55)	(340) 692-0524
Ace Roti Shop	Lunch ($15)	(340) 719-7684
Balter	Dinner ($45), Dinner ($55)	(340) 719-5896
Beach Side Café	Dinner ($35), Dinner ($45)	(340) 772-1266
Bes Craft Cocktail Lounge	Dinner ($35)	(340) 773-2985
Brew Pub	Lunch ($15)	(340) 719-6339
Cast Iron Pot	Dinner ($35)	(340) 692-2477
CHOP	Lunch ($15), Dinner ($35)	(340) 778-2467

Chris Hideaway Sport Bar and Restaurant	Lunch ($15), Dinner ($35)	(340) 64
Cultured Pelican Ristorante	Dinner ($35)	(340) 773-3333
Galangal	Dinner ($35), Dinner ($55)	(340) 773-0076
Ital in Paradise	Lunch ($15)	(340) 713-4825
J & V Diner	Lunch ($15), Lunch ($20)	(340) 773-3463
J And W Grocery/ Diner	Lunch ($15)	(340) 713-8100
Junie's	Lunch ($15), Dinner ($35)	(340) 773-2801
Kathleen's Bar & Restaurant	Lunch ($15), Lunch ($20)	(340) 713-9688
La Reine Chicken Shack	Lunch ($15)	(340) 778-5717
Luncheria	Lunch ($15)	(340) 773-4247
Roadside BBQ & Grill		(340) 227-5975
Savant	Dinner ($45)	(340) 713-8666
Seahorse Republic	Lunch ($15), Lunch ($20)	(617) 800-4942
Thali Indian Grill	Dinner ($35), Dinner ($45), Dinner ($55)	(340) 277-1642
The Galleon	Dinner ($45)	(340) 718-9948
The Mermaid at The Buccaneer	Lunch ($20)	(340) 712-2100

The Terrace at The Buccanneer	Dinner ($55)	(340) 712-2100
Toast	Lunch ($15), Lunch ($20), Dinner ($35)	(340) 692-0313
Turtles Deli	Lunch ($20)	(340) 772-3676
Twin City	Lunch ($15)	(340) 773-9400
Un Amore	Dinner ($35)	(340) 692-9922
Villa Morales	Lunch ($20), Dinner ($35)	(340) 772-0556
Zeny's Restaurant	Lunch ($15)	(340) 773-4393
Zion Modern Kitchen	Dinner ($45)	(340) 773-9466

GoToStCroix.com will continue to provide information and details on the Dine VI events and participating restaurants as they become available.

Building balter, Christiansted's Newest Restaurant

If you have been to Christiansted recently you have undoubtedly seen the construction taking place at the intersection of Company Street and Queen Cross Street. Here, in the heart of historic downtown Christiansted, an original 250 year old building is being restored and converted into the island's most anticipated new restaurant - balter. As a collaboration between award-winning chef Digby Stridiron and award-winning sommelier Patrick Kralik, balter is in a promising position to live up to the hype it is already generating.

Scheduled to open in early April, with a possible soft opening at the end of March, balter plans to focus both it's food and beverage menus around fresh, locally sourced ingredients. Staying true to his Crucian roots, Chef Digby Stridiron is crafting menus that will offer creatively composed contemporary West Indian dishes utilizing old-fashioned techniques. If you are not familiar with Chef Digby, he was born on St. Croix and is the "Culinary Ambassador of the US Virgin Islands." He makes a point to establish sustainable working relationships with the local farmers because growing up here on the island increased his awareness of the importance of locally sourcing ingredients whenever possible. Chef Digby is an official member of the Slow Food Movement and the James Beard Foundation, and he hopes that balter will make St. Croix a culinary travel destination here in the Caribbean.

When it comes to using local ingredients, it's not just about the food at balter. The bars (yes, there will be two!) will offer a "Farm to Glass" program which will utilize locally sourced, unique island ingredients in house-made craft cocktails. In fact, balter will even be bottling some of their house-made cocktails for retail purchase. With sommelier Patrick Kralik designing the bar menu, you can also expect an exquisite wine list. In fact, balter will feature varietal specific glassware and a Cruvinet system (a temperature controlled system keeps wines as fresh as the moment they are uncorked for up to six weeks) which will allow for a nice menu of wines by the glass, or by the ounce. As Patrick told me when pointing out the benefits of the Cruvinet system: "We can have very expensive wines that guests can taste by the ounce. I mean how often do you get to try a $1000 bottle of wine?"

As for the restaurant itself, balter is designed to offer both elegant indoor seating, as well as beautiful courtyard seating. The indoor and outdoor areas will each have their own bar, as well as different menus. Inside, the dining room will offer the more upscale dining experience, and will also house a retail space where guests can purchase balter's homemade ready-to-cook pastas, chutneys and sauces. For those who wish to dine alfresco, the courtyard area will be surrounded by balter's onsite gardens, and will house a stage for live music and a community table. The balter building has been designed to keep the facade and building structure in it's original Danish style, but has been repainted and is being renovated with all modern conveniences inside. The design also incorporates some of the original building materials into the renovated space, as well as adding native and locally made accessories and details wherever possible including beautiful mahogany beams, a Danish brick oven, and custom plates handmade by Don Schnell of St. John.

I don't know about you, but my mouth waters at the mere thought of enjoying one of Chef Digby's creations paired with one of Patrick's unique craft cocktails. Currently, balter is slated to be open Tuesdays - Saturdays for dinner from 6pm - 10pm, with the bar being open from 4pm - 11pm; and, Sundays for brunch from 11am - 4pm, with the bar open until 6pm. Stayed tuned to GoToStCroix.com for updates on the opening of this unique new restaurant. In the meantime, you can see a sample menu for balter, learn more about the balter family, and follow the progress of their building on their website at: www.balterstx.com.

Location : Christiansted

Phone : (340) 719-5896

Website : www.balterstx.com

balter delivers the perfect combination of simple elegance. Taste St. Croix in the offerings from balter's menu which include fresh, locally sourced ingredients in the creatively composed Contemporary West

Indian dishes created by award-winning chef, Digby Stridiron. Enjoy inspired craft cocktails, or choose from balter's extensive list of wines, thoughtfully selected by Sommelier Patrick Kralik. With unparalleled service, balter is the new standard when it comes to Crucian hospitality. Dine alfresco in balter's beautiful garden courtyard, or enjoy the air-conditioned comfort of their elegant dining room each offering their own distinct menu. Please call for reservations.

Enjoy Fresh, Local Seafood on St. Croix

Getting your fill of freshly caught, local seafood while on St. Croix is a must! The beautiful Caribbean Sea that surrounds the island offers up a variety of delicious saltwater fish and shellfish that thrive in this tropical climate. While you likely find salmon and shrimp on the menu anywhere in the world, St. Croix offers seafood delights such as Caribbean spiny lobster, red snapper, wahoo, mahi mahi, kingfish, and conch. Catch and cook your own fish, or leave it to the professionals chefs at one of the island's many delectable restaurants, just make sure you don't miss out on some fresh St. Croix seafood.

While I love to cook, I must admit that I prefer to have my fish or lobster caught, cleaned, and cooked by someone else. If you are the same way, St. Croix has a multitude of restaurants that offer seafood prepared in both traditional and inventive ways. Traditional island preparations of locally caught seafood include conch in butter sauce, fried kingfish, stewed 'potfish' (various reef fish), and kallaloo. Saltfish is a must-try while you are on island since it is a staple of the traditional Crucian breakfast, which usually consists of saltfish, johnny cakes, and cooked greens (such as spinach). If you are craving fresh lobster, many of the local restaurants offer lobster in a variety of forms from lobster benedict and seafood pastas, to whole lobster tail dinners with all the fixings. Most restaurants here on St. Croix also take advantage of the fresh mahi mahi and wahoo and feature these local catches in everything from ceviche and sashimi, to blackened or grilled entrees with delectable sauces.

Any given day on St. Croix you can find fresh seafood offerings on local restaurant menus that were likely caught that morning; but, if you enjoy fishing, you can always catch your own. There are several inshore and offshore fishing charters here on St. Croix that will take you out where you can reel in your own dinner! Fish for wahoo, mahi mahi, bonefish, kingfish, marlin, tuna and snapper with local guides who know the best fishing spots on the island. If you are staying in accommodations that allow you to cook your own meals, you can also buy fish and seafood from the local fisherman you see along the roadside. They will often have lobster and conch, when it's in season. You can also visit the Saturday farmers market in La Reine where many of the fisherman sell their catch, but you have to be there really early to get the best selection.

Whatever your seafood pleasure, the island's fantastic ocean fare that is sure to please any palette. Make sure you don't miss a single opportunity to enjoy the bounty of seafood St. Croix has to offer. Bon appetit!

Sun, Sand, and a Drink in Your Hand

Nothing evokes a sense of paradise like lying in a lounge chair on a pristine resort beach with a cold, tropical cocktail in your hand. If you are here on St. Croix you are in luck, there are a number of resorts island wide offer just such an opportunity for pure bliss. Let the sun warm your skin, feel the sand between your toes, and taste some of the tropical libations the island has to offer.

First step, find a spot to lounge. While all of the beaches on St. Croix are technically public, the beauty of utilizing resort beaches are the amenities. If you are a guest at a resort the beach side amenities will likely be offered to you as part of your stay; however, for non-guests many resorts offer use of their facilities for a small fee, or with a food or beverage purchase. If you are looking for true relaxation, believe me it will be worth paying for the amenities. In addition to close parking, restrooms, and beach side bars and restaurants, many resorts also have lounge chairs, umbrellas or cabanas, some even offer beach side food and beverage service. This saves you the hassle of packing up a beach chair and cooler, and hauling everything from wherever you can find parking to the beach. In addition to the amenities, resort beaches are kept clean and pristine by the resort staff, making them even more beautiful. Included below are links to some resorts that are great spots to spend a day lounging.

Once you have settled into your ideal beach side spot, the next step is tricky...which cocktail shall you choose? If you want to taste the local flavors, try a rum based cocktail like a Dark and Stormy, Rum Punch, Mango Mojito, or a Cruzan Confusion. Both Cruzan Rum and Captain Morgan Rum are distilled here on St. Croix, so the list of rum drinks available is limitless! Another local favorite cocktail is the Bailey's Banana Colada (or BBC), a decadent frozen drink featuring Baileys Irish Cream, rum, banana liqueur, fresh banana, and Coco Lopez. If you are a fan of the dessert-like frozen cocktails, you may also want to try a Bushwacker or a Lime in da Coconut. For something deliciously fruity, but a little lighter enjoy a fresh mango or banana daiquiri. For those that prefer beer, you can find a variety of foreign and domestic beers as well. Don't worry, all of the resorts also offer great virgin drink options for those who want the tropical experience without the alcohol.

Now for the final and most important step, sit back and relax! Sip your drink and let the Caribbean experience wash over you. This is the way paradise was meant to be experienced, so enjoy a leisurely day on St. Croix with the sun, sand, and a drink in your hand.

Plants and Animals

Many different species of plants and animals call St. Croix home, thanks to the diverse landscape of the island. As you make your way around the island, you are likely to see mongoose crossing the roads, iguanas sunning near the beach, Senepol cattle grazing alongside the road, and a vast array of birds fishing along the shore or diving into the water. In the waters of Caribbean Sea itself is a whole different ecosystem complete with an unimaginable amount of tropical fish, turtles, other animals, corals and vast amounts of plant life. And don't forget the rainforest with it's lush trees and dense foliage. Learn about the native plants and animals of St. Croix by visiting the botanical gardens and/or local farms, or by reading the information provided here on our website!

Insects & Bugs

While many people are not big fans of bugs, St. Croix is an entemologist's dream! Yes, we have those pesky mosquitoes, but the island is also host to a number of wonderfully strange and sometime even beautiful insects and bugs. For example, if you look in the frangipani trees you may spot the colorful sphinx moth caterpillars munching on leaves. As you make your way around the island you will see lots of colorful little butterflies and moths fluttering around the flowers and bushes. You may even be fortunate enough to find some of the well camouflaged walking stick bugs or green stink bugs, which look like a little green leaves. Keep your eyes open, you never know what you may find!

Sphinx Moth Caterpillars
Sphinx Moth Caterpillars are large, brightly striped yellow and black caterpillars with bright red heads. A full grown larvae can grow up to 10 inches long! Amazingly, when they develop into their adult stage, they are small moth that is brownish in color. You can usually find groups of these caterpillars eating the leaves off of frangipani trees.

No-See-Ums
This is the official, technical term for little nat-like bugs that you can't see, but you can certainly feel! They itch like the devil and like damp, moist, low-lying outside areas. You might also encounter noseeums on the beach around dusk. Wear long pants when dining at certain outside restaurants. They are also referred to as Sandflys

Mosquitoes
Unfortunately, mosquitoes are a harsh reality of life in the tropics. Mosquitoes are usually prevalent after big rains, and feed at dawn and

dusk. There is no way to eradicate them, so come prepared! Here on St. Croix mosquitoes can carry some viruses such as dengue fever and chikungunya, so do your best to avoid being bitten. Bring your favorite non-aerosol bug spray, bug repellant wipes, garlic water or what ever concoction you desire just in case you think you might be a target. Most hotels, bars and restaurants on St. Croix can provide repellant if you need it. Keep a fan running at night to circulate the air and keep the mosquitoes at bay.

Animals & Birds

By land or by sky, the island of St. Croix is home to a variety of creatures. The rainforest and bush are home to unique animals like the mongoose, iguanas, and even hermit crabs. The island's agricultural scene breeds domesticated animals such as horses, goats, sheep, and Senepol cattle as well as the often seen chickens. Many visitors are surprised to find that deer have even found a home here on St. Croix. Birdwatchers are thrilled to find that the skies, land and coastline are home to a multitude of birds including pelicans, egrets, kestrels, hummingbirds, and our beautiful state bird, the bananaquit. As you enjoy your time on St. Croix, make sure you take in the diverse wildlife the island has to offer...it is everywhere.

St. Croix 'Animal Jam' Raises Funds for Animal Welfare

One of my favorite things about St. Croix from day one has been the way that most people here truly treat their pets like a member of the family (as they should). Unfortunately, like many places worldwide, St. Croix has a problem with pet overpopulation so, not all of our pets have a family. The good news is that we have five different organizations here on the island working hard every day to help care for and find homes for homeless pets, to educate people on the pet overpopulation issue, and to be advocates for animal rights and the humane treatment of animals.

Here is a little bit of information about these organizations and how Animal Jam is helping to raise funds for these organizations:

St. Croix Animal Welfare Center: As the only animal shelter facility servicing St. Croix, SCAWC provides care to thousands of dogs and cats each year. They fulfill the Territory contract for animal control, and provide animal abuse response and investigation in collaboration with VIPD. They also adopt out hundreds of animals locally and off island via their transfer program 'Pets from Paradise'. They strive to break the cycle of neglect and promote responsible pet ownership via their humane educational outreach to schools and adults. However, even with their government allotment they are grossly underfunded, and their nonprofit organization is in financial crisis.

Healing Paws Sanctuary: The HPS is being created to provide a safe place for homeless and unwanted animals whether they have been abandoned, neglected, abused or without a home. HPS will try to care for and heal them until they can find a 'forever home' for these animals.

Sunshine Foundation: The Sunshine Foundation is dedicated to ending pet overpopulation on St Croix by providing basic, high-volume/low-cost spay and neuter services to people and pets in need. At this time, their focus is on Feral Cats, and there goal is to encourage widespread community participation and a team effort in seeing this mission fulfilled.

Cruzan Cowgirls Horse Rescue: Cruzan Cowgirls intends to provide visitors to the island of St Croix with the unique and exciting experience of horseback riding in one of the most beautiful places in the world. It was created to generate income that will be used to benefit the homeless and abused horses on St Croix and as a platform to educate the public about the plight of these horses. All of our horses are rehabilitated rescues who are being given a second chance at a much better life where they are deeply loved by our family, our community and our visitors.

VI Humane Learning Center: The VI Humane Learning Center's Humane Education team works hard to visit every school with different presentations for each grade that focus on responsible pet care, safety around animals, the importance of spay and neuter and the connection between animal cruelty and interpersonal violence. We use the care of animals and the understanding of animal needs to promote values of justice, kindness, and mercy, not only to animals, but to each other.

These organizations have all joined forces to raise funds in a truly Crucian way, by throwing a beach party! The Animal Jam is held at Rhythms at Rainbow Beach. This event offers live music all day long, games, family activities, water sports, raffles, a beach bar and, most importantly, showcases St. Croix's animal welfare organizations and provide information to the public on how they can help! There is a SCAWC Doggie Parade, as well as information booths, and plenty of adoptable pets no doubt. The entry fee is only $10 per adult, $5 for children 12-17, and children under 12 are free! All proceeds from this event benefit animal welfare here on St. Croix.

Animal Jam is a fun day for the whole family, so attend this annual event and support these amazing animal welfare organizations and all the good work they do. All you have to do is come out to the Animal Jam and have some fun, hear some great live music, play with the pets, and learn how you can do your part to help the animals of St. Croix!

In addition to Animal Jam, here are a few ways you can help the animals here on St. Croix:

- ✓ Spay/neuter your pets!

- ✓ Adopt your next pet

- ✓ Donate to one of the island's five animal welfare/rescue organizations. To make a donation now, please visit the Animal Jam donation page.

- ✓ Volunteer your time to one of the animal welfare organizations

- ✓ Foster a rescued animal

- ✓ Sponsor a Pet from Paradise

- ✓ Report animal neglect and abuse

- ✓ Take a class at The Blue Mutt

- ✓ Shop at The Blue Mutt or the St. Croix Animal Welfare Fleamarket

Senepol Cattle

Senepol Cattle are a beautiful species of cattle that is native to St. Croix. The feed on the lush green hills on the west end of the island. This breed of cattle was bred to stand up to island conditions such as drought and heat. Two major working cattle farms still exist on St. Croix, Castle Nugent Farm and Annaly Farm.

Mongoose

Mongoose are like the curious little mascot of St. Croix. Mongoose is the popular English name species in the 14 genera of the Herpestidae family , which are small carnivorans that are native to southern Eurasia and mainland Africa. You'll catch these quick little rodents scurrying across the road, or even taunting an iguana. Mongoose were brought to the island to eradicate the rat problem. Well, problem was, rats were nocturnal (they like the night time) and mongoose are diurnal (they like the day time); which means that little plan didn't work out so well.

Iguanas

IguanasLook in trees, mangroves and scurrying across the road for this pre-historic looking reptile. Iguanas are native to the Caribbean where they like the sun and warm waters just as much as Look in trees, mangroves and scurrying across the road for this pre-historic looking reptile. Iguanas are native to the Caribbean where they like the sun and warm waters just as much as you do! Babies are brightly colored and FAST! Adult males can be dark green or blue and can grow up to six feet long. Females tend to be less colorful in grays and browns. On St. Croix, you most likely find iguanas at Tamarind Beach and Salt River. Please do not feed them; just observe them from afar!

Hermit Crabs

First thing's first: do not take these cute crustaceans home to keep as a pet. They live here for a reason. When the animal that lives inside the hard shell grows, he searches for and moves into a new, larger home! You can find hermit crabs on the outskirts of the beach, but also in thick vegetation areas known as The Bush. You'll here them walking and rolling down the hills if you hike in the rainforest.

Gecko

Commonly referred to as a House Gecko; they are EVERYWHERE on St. Croix! Geckos are cute, fun to watch and totally harmless. In fact, people allow them to stay in their homes because they eat the bugs!

Donkeys

Donkeys were brought here by colonists from under every flag. They are traditionally work animals. On St. John, you might be awakened in the middle of the night by the breigh of a feral donkey wandering in the bush. On St. Croix, no feral donkeys, but you can see them during parades and even Donkey Races!

Deer

Yep, deer on the island. They were brought here in the 1700's for sport. No hunting is allowed of these gentle animals. They exist from the east to the west ends of St. Croix and are much smaller than their stateside cousins

Chickens

A.K.A. Yard Birds. These cluckers are pretty much feral and run amuck all over the island. You'll see them in town, hens with chicks, roosters crowing. Some locals do care and feed for them, and even collect their eggs and provide a safe place to roost. For the most part, it is just plain fun so catch a glimpse of these crazy bird.

Bats

BatsRight at dusk, you can catch glimpses of these fast-flying mammals. They fly out from under roof eaves, caves, and even abandoned structures to feed on insects; which really helps

Bats

Right at dusk, you can catch glimpses of these fast-flying mammals. They fly out from under roof eaves, caves, and even abandoned structures to feed on insects; which really helps keeps the mosquito population down! If you are relaxing by the pool, you might even see them skim the water. No need to be afraid, our bats are strictly vegetarian and have no interest in sucking your blood.

Fish & Sealife

Being surrounded by the warm Caribbean Sea, St. Croix offers a vast array of fish and sealife. Schools of tropical fish mingle around the colorful coral reefs, dolphins play in the deeper waters, and octopus hide among the rocks and bits of coral. St. Croix is a well known haven for nesting sea turtles including the green, hawksbill, and the massive leatherback sea turtle varieties. For several months out of the year humpback whales even migrate through the waters off the coast of the North Shore. To get a closer look at the diverse sea life St. Croix has to offer, you can dive or snorkel with these amazing fish and sea creatures in their natural habitat, so even enjoy a peak at some of them from shore.

Plants & Flowers

As you take in the beauty of St. Croix, you will see that beautiful flora abounds on the island. In many cases, you may find yourself wondering what some of the plants are and how they came to be on this island. Thanks to St. Croix's diverse landscapes, from the lush rainforest of the West End to arid desert-like East End, the island is home to plants ranging in nature from tropical flowering vines to spiny cactus and everything in between. If you find yourself looking for information on what some of the unique and beautiful plants of St. Croix are, where they come from, if they are edible, or if they have any medicinal or practical uses, please check out our Plant Guide.

Tan Tan

This prolific plant can be found almost everywhere on the island. It grows fast and thick, starting as a small twig and eventually, if left alone, can grow to a great size. In the Virgin Islands tan tan plants usually reach between 15 and 20 feet tall. It's branches are covered with little green oval leaves and leaflets that fold up with heat, cold or lack of water. It produces white flowers year round in dense, round balls and is sporadically filled with clusters of flat green, then brown, pods, each about 6 inches long. Inside the pods are numerous shiny seeds, changing color with the pod, in a ladder-like linear series. The stems have no thorns, which makes the pods easy to get to. Although this bush can be considered a nuisance, it is a nitrogen fixer, which helps to build the soil. However, it also contains an alkaloid, which over a period of time, can cause loss of long hair in livestock.

Tan tan harms the local environment by displacing native vegetation. A stand of tan tan often has few other species interspersed within it and provides low quality wildlife habitat, largely because the flower and fruit are not food for wildlife.

Practical Uses:

The tan tan seeds can be strung into quite interesting and unique necklaces. Young tan tan leaves and seeds can be used as vegetables for human consumption. Young green pods can be split open and the fresh immature seeds eaten raw or cooked; however, only small amounts can be eaten in this way because of the presence of the toxic amino acid mimosine

Century Plant

Although it is called the century plant, it typically lives only 10 to 30 years. It has a spread of about 6 to 10 feet with gray-green leaves of 3 to 5 feet. The century plant resembles an aloe plant, except it is much larger and possesses sharper spines on the leaves' edges and its pointed tip is sharp and strong. Until flowering, each plant has a single stem bud which produces leaves in clusters near the ground. When the plant has stored enough food, usually after a decade or so, the stem bud starts to grow this is called 'flowering'. At flowering, the main stem elongates rapidly to reach a total height of up to 25 to 30 feet. Flowers grow in lateral groups of tubular, 6-parted yellow clusters that look like upturned candelabras. When it is done, it dies and the whole plant dies with it, although a new plant usually sprouts from the roots.

Practical Uses:

If the flower stem is cut without flowering, a sweet liquid called aguamiel (or honey water) gathers in the heart of the century plant which may be fermented to produce the drink called pulque. In the tequila-producing regions of Mexico, agaves (such as the century plant) are called mezcales and their nectar is distilled to make mezcal. Agave nectar, also called agave syrup, is a product of the century plant and is marketed as a natural form of sugar due to its high fructose content. The leaves of the century plant also yield fibers, known as pita, which are suitable for making rope, matting, coarse cloth, and are used for embroidery of leather in a technique known as piteado.

Medicinal Uses:

The century plant yields a sap that is employed medicinally as a laxative and a diuretic. The juice, extracted from the leaves of the plant, is applied externally on bruises and is also ingested for treating a number of problems related to the gastric tract including constipation, indigestion and dysentery. In addition, the juice of the leaves is also said to be an effective remedy for jaundice. Precursors of steroid hormones are also derived from the century plant leaves.

Casha Bush

Native to:

The native range is uncertain. While the point of origin is Mexico and Central America, the species has a pantropical distribution incorporating northern Australia and southern Asia.

Description:

This very intimidating thorn-covered bush is seen almost everywhere on St. Croix. The species grows to a height of up to 26 feet and has a lifespan of about 25 to 50 years. Its leaves are numerous, each about an inch long and blunt tipped. The casha bush also holds tiny spherical yellow flowers and a nearly cylindrical legume pod, 4 to 5 inches long. The stem is thin and woody, usually contorted and covered with whitish thorns an inch or more long on mature stems. Be careful when hiking, as the casha thorns can do some damage to exposed knees, legs, and feet.

Practical Uses:

The seeds are not toxic to humans and are a valuable food source for people throughout the plant's range. The leaves are used as a tamarind flavoring for chutneys and the pods are roasted to be used in sweet and sour dishes. The flowers are processed through distillation to produce a perfume called Cassie, which is widely used in the perfume industry in Europe. A black pigment is extracted from the bark and fruit and used in inks and dyes. The wood of the cashsa bush is very hard making it an excellent tree for making charcoal.

Medicinal Uses:

The bark and the flowers are the parts of the tree most used in traditional medicine. Casha bush has been used to treat malaria, and the extract from the tree bark and leaves has shown some efficacy against the malarial pathogen in animal models . The roots and bark of the tree are used to treat diarrhea and diseases of the skin. The tree's leaves can also be rubbed on the skin to treat skin diseases

Cactus

Cactus (Echinocactus grusonii)

Many different types of cacti are present throughout St.Croix, mostly on the dry terrain of the East End. The "prickly pear" (a) can be found throughout the island. Many use it for it's decorative properties. This particular cactus possesses jointed stems formed of flattened segments covered with hairs. The flowers are yellow or orange, sometimes blushed red near the base. The fruits are purple. During harvesting, gloves can be worn to avoid being wounded by the spines and hairs. The sweet fruit is usually eaten raw, alone or placed in fruit salads. The Turks Cap (b) is completely covered with spines, has a short, stubby, barrel-like bottom with a taller, cylindrical top usually red and bristly. It can grow as large as 30 cm in height by 8 cm in diameter. Pink flowers develop among the bristles and spines so it makes for a great ornamental cactus. It thrives in arid, rocky areas along the coasts. Night-Blooming Cactus (c) is flaccid with a diameter of 1 to 3 cm, and usually requires the stability of another plant, so it is often found wrapped and hanging from other plants. It grows as a vining shrub with fleshy stems that are covered with silky spines up to 1.5 cm long and with deciduous white or yellow hairs. At night the white flowers bloom. Native to Jamaica, the Cayman Islands, and Cuba, it inhabits the scrub woods near the coast. It has been sold throughout the states for its ornamental purpose, and is also subject to large-scale cultivation since it yields a medicinal substance that stimulates the cardiovascular system. The Pipe Organ cactus (d) also commonly seen throughout the east end of the island stands tall and thin and is covered with woody, needle-like spines, varying in lengths to 2 inches long. Fluting is an adaptation to provide the plant with a greater green surface.

Aloe Vera

Scientific & Common Name:

Aloe vera, commonly known as Chinese aloe, Indian aloe, true aloe, burn aloe, first aid plant

Native to:

The natural range of aloe vera is unclear, as the species has been widely cultivated throughout the world; however, it is believed to have originated on the Mediterranean coast of Africa.

Description:

Aloe thrives in climates such as the Caribbean as well as Central and South America. It has large, fleshy, grayish-green, strap-like leaves close to the ground edged with spines and a pointed tip. Aloe vera grows to about 24 to 39 inches tall. The aloe vera flowers in the summer on a spike up to 35 inches tall, each flower being pendulous, with a yellow tubular corolla about an inch long.

Practical Uses:

In the Virgin Islands, the external uses are numerous. It is used as an emollient, a bath, hair conditioner, and sunscreen. When stewed, aloe has immense benefits to the hair, nails, and especially skin. In South America, it is often worn as a mosquito repellent, and whole plants hung upside down to repel insects.

Medicinal Uses:

Aloe is used frequently in the treatment of burns, cuts, and sores. Internally, it has been used for the treatments of colds and fevers, coughs, and intestinal worms. Aloe vera juice is also marketed to support the health of the digestive system.

Plumbago

Plumbago (Plumbago capensis)

Also called Leadwort because of its lead colored roots. Plumbago can be found growing wildly along the roadside or in planters around the island as decoration.In clusters among simple, elliptical leaves, the flowers are a light blue or lavender color. Each flower is 5 parted, long and tubular, with a distinctive mid-vein. The tube of each flower is covered with sticky hairs, making it easy for the flowers to rest in one's hair or clothes for a little island color.These hairs aid in seed dispersal. This plant, grown as a very colorful hedge, should be pruned vigorously to reduce its sprawl. Because it is native to South Africa, Plumbago accepts our full sun and tropical heat.

Hibiscus

Hibiscus (Hibiscus spp)

Because of its great beauty and hardiness, the Hibiscus has become a well-known and well-loved plant. It may be the official flower of Hawaii, but the Hibiscus can be seen in the Virgin Islands growing wildly along the roadside, or elegantly covering a window by someone's home. Its presence is also seen in the states, unfortunately, during winter month's, it can only thrive indoors. There are many different species of this beauty, one being from Asia, the Hibiscus rosa-sinensis, and one from East Africa, the Hibiscus schizopetalus. Hibiscus rosa-sinensis has leaves that are simple and broadly oval.

They narrow into a point and are about 3 to 6 inches long. Blooms are solitary, enormous, 5-parted and come in colors of red, orange, pink, yellow, lavender, or white. Less common are combinations of these colors. Schizopetalus, has coarsely toothed leaves, narrowing outward into a point, and a shorter stalk with a somewhat wavy surface. Flowers are a pale red. The 5 petals are bent back, deeply and repeatedly cut and curved into a striking display. They are very similar to one another, except the schizopetalus has leaves that are more distantly spaced, and the branches are more delicate.

The flower from any Hibiscus, whether on or off the plant, will remain fresh all day, and then wilt in the evening. A dye obtained from the red petals, though useful, will stain clothes. The petals of the Hibiscus can also be boiled, sweetened and made into a tea. A cutting from this hardy plant, when placed in water for a few weeks, will readily root. Locally, these plants are attacked and harmed by tiny white insects. Green Tea, steeped and sprayed on the infected leaves, helps to rid these pests without the use of chemicals.

Ginger Thomas

Ginger Thomas (The USVI Official Flower)

Native to tropical and subtropical America, Texas, New Mexico and Florida, this beautiful yellow flower can be found thriving year round on St. Croix from hillsides and thickets alike. Ginger Thomas is so abundant that it is considered our territory's flower. Not only is it a pleasure to look at, but historically, it has proved to have great medicinal value. The leaves of the Ginger Thomas are used to reduce fever and to strengthen a woman's body after childbirth. The leaves have also been known to ease symptoms of the common cold, diabetes, headaches, and high blood pressure, while the roots have been used to ease symptoms of syphilis. Take a moment to smell the flowers! The scent is fragrant, like that of champagne.

Frangipani

Scientific & Common Names:
Solandra nitida, are commonly know as cup of gold, trumpt flower, or chalice vines

Native to:

The Caribbean, Mexico, Central and South Americas

Description:
Cup of gold is a striking vine with glossy leaves and large showy white to bright yellow flowers that are 6 to 8 inches long and are chalice shaped. They have a yellow corolla , with 5 purple lines. Cup of gold blooms intermittently through the year, usually from February until May. The thick and woody ropelike stems branch frequently and root at their nodes, and can run for more than 30 to 40 feet, clinging with aerial rootlets and scrambling over everything in the way. The evergreen leaves are leathery, about 6 inches long and elliptic, with prominent lighter colored midribs and lateral veins. They are fragrant, especially at night, with a scent reminiscent of coconut. The fruits,

rarely seen in cultivation, are round berries, about 2 inches in diameter.

Medicinal Uses:

In Mexico, the cup of gold is used in folk medicine, primarily as a love drink and aphrodisiac. The Huastec use the rainwater or dew that has collected in the buds of the cup of gold as eye drops to improve sight. A tea made from the flowers is also drunk to treat coughing

Cup of Gold

Scientific & Common Names:
Solandra nitida, are commonly known as cup of gold, trumpt flower, or chalice vines

Native to:

The Caribbean, Mexico, Central and South Americas

Description:
Cup of gold is a striking vine with glossy leaves and large showy white to bright yellow flowers that are 6 to 8 inches long and are chalice shaped. They have a yellow corolla, with 5 purple lines. Cup of gold blooms intermittently through the year, usually from February until May. The thick and woody ropelike stems branch frequently and root at their nodes, and can run for more than 30 to 40 feet, clinging with

aerial rootlets and scrambling over everything in the way. The evergreen leaves are leathery, about 6 inches long and elliptic, with prominent lighter colored midribs and lateral veins. They are fragrant, especially at night, with a scent reminiscent of coconut. The fruits, rarely seen in cultivation, are round berries, about 2 inches in diameter.

Medicinal Uses:
In Mexico, the cup of gold is used in folk medicine, primarily as a love drink and aphrodisiac. The Huastec use the rainwater or dew that has collected in the buds of the cup of gold as eye drops to improve sight. A tea made from the flowers is also drunk to treat coughing

Crown of Thorns

Scientific & Common Names:
Euphorbia milii, commonly known as crown of thorns, Christ plant, Christ thorn

Native to:

Madagascar

Description:
Crown of thorns is a succulent climbing shrub growing up to 5 feet tall. It's blooms are mostly red and its thick stems are covered in thorns. The straight, slender spines, up to 1 inch long, help it scramble over

other plants.Cuttings from this plant can be stuck directly in the soil and grow with out an existing root system. The leaves are found mainly on new growth, and are green and tear-shaped, up to 1 inch long and half an inch broad.

Practical Uses:
The latex of some crown of thorn species has been used for arrow poisons and to stupefy fish for capture. Euphorbia plants are also used as food by the larvae of some Lepidoptera (butterflies and moths), like the Spurge Hawk-moths, as well as the Giant Leopard Moth.

Medicinal Uses:
Despite its poisonous properties, in the past the latex has also been used for medicinal purposes. The Chinese use it as a cure for cancer, and some Brazilians believe that it can cure warts.

Toxicity:
The sap is moderately poisonous, and causes irritation on contact with skin or eyes. If ingested, it causes severe stomach pain, irritation of the throat and mouth, and vomiting. Honey made from the flowers of these plants may be toxic.

Bougainvillea
Scientific & Common Names:

Bougainvillea spectabilis, of the Nyctaginaceae family, is commonly known as bougainvillea

Native to:

South America

Description:

Bougainvillea is a tropical and subtropical woody, evergreen, shrubby vine. Typically multi-trunked or with clumping stems, it has a spreading, round plant habit with a height and spread of up to 20 feet. It climbs by sending out slender arching canes armed with stiff curved thorns. Leaves are small, elliptical, and become narrow to a point. Paper-like flowers grow in clusters of bright colors ranging from a dark pink or purple to a subtle white. Enclosed inside each paper-like case is a single, tiny, tubular, white flower. This plant is named after Louis de Bougainville, a French navigator. While in Brazil, he found these beautiful plants and brought them back to his home in Europe for cultivation. They readily root from cuttings, prefer full sun, and can withstand drought as well as heavy pruning. When admiring these beauties, be careful not to grab a hold of their stem because of the large, widely spaced thorns.

Toxicity:

The sap of the bougainvillea can cause serious skin rashes

Bird of Paradise

Scientific & Common Names:
Strelitzia, more commonly known as the bird of paradise or crane flower

Native to:

South Africa

Description:
The bird of paradise is actually a large tropical herb that is a member of the banana family which typically reaches 5 to 10 feet tall. It's large leaves are 12 to 79 inches long and 4 to 30 inches broad, similar to a banana leaf in appearance but with a longer petiole, and arranged strictly in two ranks to form a fan-like crown of evergreen foliage. The flower stalks are actually a combination of blue petals and orange petal-looking leaves that emerge from a beak-like leaf structure. The species was brought to the Caribbean because of its beauty and its ability to do well in our warm, humid climate

Trees & Fruit

St. Croix is home to wide variety of trees, thanks in large part to our multicultural heritage and diverse landscapes. In addition to native tropical trees, you will find many trees that have made their way to St.

Croix from places like Africa, North America, Central and South America, and the West Indies. On the West End of St. Croix, the lush rainforest is filled with towering kapok and baobab trees, as well as countless tropical fruit trees. The scenic shorelines of the island are dotted with palm trees, manchineel, and seaside mahoe. Island wide you will find ancient mahogany trees, tamarind trees, and a variety of colorful and vibrant flowering trees like the African tulip tree. Many of the trees on the island are used for medicinal or practical applications, or as food sources. For anyone interested in learning more about the trees found on St. Croix, our Tree Guide offers basic information, photos, and uses for some of the trees you will see across the island.

Sugar Apple

Scientific & Common Names:

Sugar apples, also known as custard apples, are the most widely grown of the *Annona* species

Native to:

The original home of the sugar apple is unknown. It is commonly cultivated in tropical South America, not often in Central America, very frequently in southern Mexico, the West Indies, Bahamas and Bermuda, and occasionally in southern Florida.

Tree Description:

The sugar apple tree requires a tropical or near-tropical climate. It ranges from 10 to 20 feet in height with an open crown of irregular branches, and somewhat zigzag twigs. Deciduous, oblong and blunt tipped leaves, are alternately arranged on short, hairy petioles, and range in size from from 2 to 6 inches long and 3/4 to 2 inches wide. The leaves are dull-green on the top side, and pale with a bloom on the bottom.

The leaves are also slightly hairy when young, and are aromatic when crushed. Along the branch tips, opposite the leaves, the fragrant flowers bloom in groups of 2 to 4. The flowers are also oblong, 1 to 1 1/2 inches in length and never fully open. They have drooping stalks, and 3 fleshy outer petals, yellow-green on the outside and pale-yellow inside with a purple or dark-red spot at the base. The compound fruit is nearly round, ovoid, or conical and is about 2 1/3 to 4 inches long.

The thick rind of the sugar apple is composed of knobby segments, generally pale-green, gray-green, or bluish-green. Many of the fruit segments enclose a single cylindrical, black or dark-brown seed about 1/2 inches long. There may be a total of 20 to 38 seeds, or more, in the average fruit; however, some trees bear seedless fruits. Seedlings 5 years old may yield 50 fruits per tree in late summer and fall. Older trees rarely exceed 100 fruits per tree unless hand-pollinated. With age, the fruits become smaller and it is considered best to replace the trees after 10 to 20 years.

Fruit Description:
When ripe, the segments of the sugar apple begin to separate and reveal the mass of conically segmented, creamy-white, glistening, delightfully fragrant, juicy, sweet, delicious flesh of the fruit. The ripe sugar apple is usually broken open and the flesh segments enjoyed while the hard seeds are separated in the mouth and spat out. It is sweet and luscious, making it well worth the trouble. The name "custard apple" comes from the fact that the flesh is creamy white to light yellow, and resembles and tastes like custard.

Sugar apple flowers | Cross section of a sugar apple

Cuisine:
While generally eaten in it's raw form, the flesh of sugar apples can be pressed through a sieve to eliminate the seeds and then added to ice cream, smoothies, or blended with milk to make a cool beverage. It is generally not cooked.

Nutrition and Practical Uses:
The sugar apple is high in vitamin C and is a moderate source of B-complex vitamins. Sugar apples also contain several poly-phenolic antioxidants, the most prominent is Annonaceous acetogenins.

Acetogenin compounds are powerful cytotoxins and have been found to have anti-cancer, anti-malarial and de-worming properties. The fiber in sugar apples is also supposed to slow down the absorption of sugar in the body, reducing the risk of Type 2 Diabetes.

Throughout tropical America, a decoction of the leaves alone or with those of other plants is imbibed either a tonic, cold remedy, digestive, or to clarify the urine. The leaf decoction is also employed in baths to alleviate rheumatic pain. In India, the crushed ripe fruit, mixed with salt, is applied on tumors. The bark and roots are both highly astringent. The bark decoction is given as a tonic and to halt diarrhea. The root, because of its strong purgative action, is administered as a drastic treatment for dysentery and other ailments.

Toxicity and Warnings:
The seeds are acrid and poisonous. In fact, powdered seeds, also pounded dried fruits serve as fish poison and insecticides in India. A paste of the seed powder has been applied to the head to kill lice but must be kept away from the eyes as it is highly irritant and can cause blindness.

Mango
Scientific & Common Names:

Mangoes (or mangos) are juicy stone fruits belonging to the genus Mangifera indica

Native to:
South Asia, first grown in India over 5,000 years ago

Plant Description:
The mango tree grows in tropical and sub-tropical climates and frost-free climates since extended exposure to temperatures below 30°F can kill or severely damage a mango tree. Mango trees can grow quite large, reaching a height of over 100 feet with a canopy of 35 feet or more, although mangoes being cultivated for harvest are often pruned and kept much smaller to be more manageable for picking. The mango tree has large, leathery leaves, five to 16 inches in length, and flowers are produced in terminal clusters about four to 16 inches long. Each flower is small with white petals and a mild, sweet aroma and less than 1% of the flowers will mature to form a fruit. It takes approximately four months for the mangoes to mature on the tree before they're ready to be harvested. Certain mangoes on each tree will receive more sunlight than others, with some fruit staying shaded within the tree's canopy. In certain varieties, the mangoes that receive the most sunlight will develop a red blush at the stem end; however, this red blush is not an indicator of maturity or ripeness.

Mango flowers starting to produce fruit

Fruit Description:
Mangoes can vary quite a bit in size and color based on the variety, and there are over 300 varieties worldwide! Mangoes are generally sweet, although the taste and texture of the flesh also varies by variety. Some mangoes have a soft, pulpy texture similar to an overripe plum, some are firmer, like a cantaloupe or avocado, and some may even have a fibrous texture. Inside the fruit is a large, flat, oblong pit which contains a single seed within. The skin of unripe, pickled, or cooked mango can be consumed, but has the potential to cause contact dermatitis of the lips or tongue in susceptible people.

It can be difficult to pick out a ripe mango based on it's color, so the best way to pick out ripe mangoes is to squeeze them gently. A ripe mango will give slightly and a firm mango will ripen at room temperature over a few days. To speed up ripening, place mangoes in a paper bag at room temperature or set them in the sun for a day or two. Once ripened, mangoes can be moved to the refrigerator to slow down ripening for several days.

Cuisine:
Mangoes are often eaten on their own, or the ripe fruit is used in used in smoothies, sorbets, or other sweet desserts. The ripe fruit is also used in savory dishes like salads, sauces, chutneys, salsas, or to top meat or fish. Mangoes also have natural tenderizing properties,

making them a perfect ingredient for marinades. The popular combination of sweet and salty, or sweet and spicy makes the mango a popular fruit in many cultures to sprinkle with chili powder, lime salt, or vinegar. Even the sour, unripe mangoes are used in things like chutneys, pickles, green mango salad, and side dishes. Due to the high natural sugar content of mangoes, they are also popular for making fermented drinks like mango wine or mead.

Nutrition and Practical Uses:
Mangoes are high in vitamin C and folate, and are a good source of natural fiber. Dried mango skin and its seeds are also used in Ayurvedic medicines. Mango leaves are used to decorate archways and doors in Indian houses and during weddings and celebrations such as Ganesh Chaturthi.

Toxicity and Warnings:
Contact with sap or the oils in mango leaves with skin can cause dermatitis and, in rarer cases, anaphylaxis in susceptible individuals (especially those with a history of dermatitis induced by contact with poison ivy, poison oak, or poison sumac). However, sensitized individuals are still able to safely eat peeled mangoes or drink mango juice.

CPSIA information can be obtained
at www.ICGtesting.com
Printed in the USA
BVOW08s1157040418
512448BV00005B/553/P